Essential Tunisia

by Peter Lilley

Above: *camels arriving at the Festival du Sahara, Douz*

PASSPORT BOOKS
NTC/Contemporary Publishing Group

Above: *local women shopping in the market at Houmt Souq*

Front cover: *15th-century fort, Houmt Souq harbour; hibiscus flowers; girl in traditional costume*
Back cover: *felted woollen hats for sale at the market*

This edition first published in 2000 by Passport Books, a division of NTC/ Contemporary Publishing Group, Inc., 4255 West Touhy Avenue, Lincolnwood (Chicago), Illinois 60712–1975 U.S.A.

Published by Passport Books in conjunction with The Automobile Association of Great Britain.

Written by Peter Lilley

Library of Congress Catalog Card Number: on file
ISBN 0-658-00630-4

Colour separation: Chroma Graphics (Overseas) Pte Ltd, Singapore

Printed and bound in Italy by Printer Trento srl

Contents

About this Book 4

Viewing Tunisia 5–14

Peter Lilley's Tunisia 6
Tunisia's Features 7
Essence of Tunisia 8–9
The Shaping of Tunisia 10–11
Peace and Quiet 12–13
Tunisia's Famous 14

Top Ten 15–26

Dougga 16
El Jem 17
Iles Kerkennah 18
Jebel Ichkeul National Park 19
Kairouan 20–1
Ksar Ouled Soltane 22
Musée du Bardo, Tunis 23
Qasr el-Aïn, Nefta 24
Sidi Bou Saïd 25
Thermes d'Antonin (Antonine Baths) 26

What to See 27–90

Tunis and the North 29–45
Cap Bon 47–55
Food and Drink 56–7
Central Tunisia 59–73
In the Know 74–5
Jerba and the South 77–90

Where To... 91–116

Eat and Drink 92–9
Stay 100–7
Shop 108–9
Take the Children 110–11
Be Entertained 112–16

Practical Matters 117–124

Index 125–6

Acknowledgements 126

About this Book

KEY TO SYMBOLS

- map reference to the maps found in the What to See section
- address or location
- telephone number
- opening times
- restaurant or café on premises or near by
- nearest underground train station
- nearest bus/tram route
- nearest overground train station
- ferry crossings and boat excursions
- travel by air
- tourist information
- facilities for visitors with disabilities
- admission charge
- other places of interest near by
- other practical information
- ➤ indicates the page where you will find a fuller description

Essential *Tunisia* is divided into five sections to cover the most important aspects of your visit to Tunisia.

Viewing Tunisia pages 5–14
An introduction to Tunisia by the author.
Tunisia's Features
Essence of Tunisia
The Shaping of Tunisia
Peace and Quiet
Tunisia's Famous

Top Ten pages 15–26
The author's choice of the Top Ten places to see in Tunisia, each with practical information.

What to See pages 27–90
The five main areas of Tunisia, each with its own brief introduction and an alphabetical listing of the main attractions.
Practical information
Snippets of 'Did you know…' information
3 suggested walks
4 suggested tours
2 features

Where To… pages 91–116
Detailed listings of the best places to eat, stay, shop, take the children and be entertained.

Practical Matters pages 117–24
A highly visual section containing essential travel information.

Maps
All map references are to the individual maps found in the What to See section of this guide.

For example, El Jem has the reference 28C5 – indicating the page on which the map is located and the grid square in which the amphitheatre is to be found. A list of the maps that have been used in this travel guide can be found in the index.

Prices
Where appropriate, an indication of the cost of an establishment is given by **£** signs:
£££ denotes higher prices, **££** denotes average prices, while **£** denotes lower charges.

Star Ratings
Most of the places described in this book have been given a separate rating:

✪✪✪	Do not miss
✪✪	Highly recommended
✪	Worth seeing

Viewing Tunisia

Peter Lilley's Tunisia	6
Tunisia's Features	7
Essence of Tunisia	8–9
The Shaping of Tunisia	10–11
Peace and Quiet	12–13
Tunisia's Famous	14

Above: *an ancient mosque above the abandoned village of Douiret*
Right: *sweet-smelling jasmine offered in Hammamet*

Peter Lilley's Tunisia

Flying Visits
There is no need to visit Tunisia for a full week or a fortnight. Easy access from Europe has increased the popularity of three- and four-night short breaks. Tunis, with more than enough attractions to interest the short-stay visitor, is a popular destination, and twinning Tunis with Hammamet makes for an exciting city/beach combination – a tonic at any time of year.

Inset: *a* médina *door studded with patterns and symbols*
Below: *men intent on a game of draughts*

Tunisia has rapidly become accepted as a mainstream Mediterranean holiday destination but it still attracts a lot of first-time visitors. In unfamiliar surroundings there is always the temptation to be cautious, trusting that the land and its people will reveal themselves in their own time: with Tunisia the secret is to immerse oneself in the culture from the moment of arrival.

If there's a choice, pick one of the early summer months and go to one of the major centres such as Tunis, Sousse or Sfax. Drop the bags and venture straight out into the streets in the late afternoon, the most magical time of day. Tunisians are at their most animated and convivial in the early evening, having been up since sunrise or soon after, and there is an infectious gaiety in the air, a sense that whatever fortunes have been won or lost, the day is over. On every street corner and scrap of rough ground, boys kick footballs and in the smoky bars and cafés this is the time for coffee, cards, chatter and *chichas* with perhaps a bottle of Celtia, Tunisia's only beer.

In the mysterious *médinas*, where skinny cats slink into every corner and there is the feeling that a thousand secrets lurk behind every studded door, shops and stalls in the *souqs* and surrounding streets spring to life to serve the homeward bound with the freshest food. Chickens are butchered to order, fish are only minutes out of the sea, bread is baked on the spot and stacks of colourful vegetables are haggled over with shouts and handshakes.

Tunisia's Features

A tradtional Bedouin band tunes up for a desert festival

Geography

• Tunisia is the northernmost country in Africa; it lies just 80km southwest of Sicily. It measures 750km from north to south but only 150km from west to east, making it slightly larger than the US state of Florida.

• The northern and eastern coastlines are bordered by the Mediterranean, while much of the southern half of the country is within the Sahara Desert.

Climate

• Summers are hot and dry. In July and August daytime temperatures on the east coast average 30°C with 12 hours of sunshine; in the desert it can reach 45°C.

• In the north, winters are mild but quite wet with occasional snow.

• Daytime temperatures in the south average 20°C but fall rapidly at night to near freezing.

People

• Tunisia has a population of just over nine million.

• More than half the population is under 18 and more than 30 per cent under 14.

• About 98 per cent of the population are Muslim with tiny Christian and Jewish minorities.

•Tunisian women enjoy considerable freedom when compared with other Muslim countries, though many older women still choose to wear the veil.

Language

• Arabic is the official language but almost everyone speaks some French.

• It is rare to find English or German spoken outside the main beach resorts.

The Berbers

The Berbers have been found in various parts of North Africa since *c*2000 BC and are generally considered to be the original Tunisians. A few centres of Berber culture survive in southern Tunisia where the people still speak the Berber language and are noted for their colourful dress, beautiful jewellery and weavings, and intricate woodcarving.

Essence of Tunisia

It would be easy to get the impression that Tunisia's only attraction is the beach resorts, and thousands of foreign visitors are drawn each year by the enticing combination of sandy beaches and sunny skies. The country also has some of the most beautiful hotels in the Mediterranean, whitewashed palaces surrounded by well-tended and spacious gardens awash with bougainvillaea. But there is much more. Even the shortest journey outside the main tourist centres reveals a fascinating and totally different culture with the quietly pervasive impact of Islam and its graceful architecture, many archaeological treasures, vivid landscapes and an exciting and varied cuisine.

Inset: *a jetskier at Zarzis beach*
Below: *visitors take to the 'ship of the desert'*

THE 10 ESSENTIALS

If you only have a short time to visit Tunisia, be sure not to leave the country without having sampled some of the essentials:

- **Buy a piece of pottery** such as an ashtray or vase, large plates or bowls. Blue and white are the traditional colours while fish decorations add extra value. Nabeul (➤ 52) and Guellala (➤ 79) are the major centres but pottery is on sale almost everywhere.
- **Eat a *brik***. This unusual egg dish is popular as a starter at lunch or dinner, but take care, it is not the easiest thing to handle!
- **Haggle** for souvenirs in a bustling *souq* especially in Tunis (➤ 35), Sousse (➤ 62) or Sfax (➤ 73). Start the bidding at around half the price you would really be prepared to pay.
- **Go to sleep** with a sweet-smelling sprig of jasmine on your pillow. Women wear garlands of the flower around their necks while men sometimes tuck one behind their ear.
- **Take a close look** at a traditional Tunisian door. Usually brightly painted, they are made of solid wood and decorated with black metal studs.
- **Ride a camel** at sunset in Douz (➤ 83), the gateway to the Sahara Desert.
- **Eat *baklava***, a honey-laced pastry filled with crushed nuts, at one of the many *pâtisseries*.
- **Listen to the *muezzin*** calling the Muslim faithful to prayer five times a day. Many mosques are closed to non-Muslims but outside prayer hours you may be able to approach as far as the door for a glimpse.
- **Visit a traditional *hammam*** (Turkish bath) and relax for an hour or two to experience one of Tunisia's great unsung pleasures.
- **Take home fresh dates**, extra virgin olive oil and a jar of fiery hot *harissa* paste.

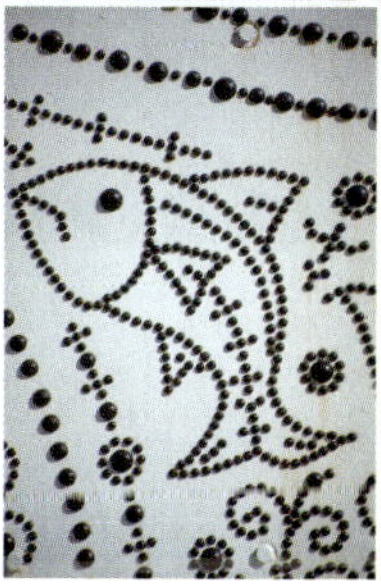

Fish are a favourite motif for use in decorative work

The Shaping of Tunisia

Dido, Queen of Carthage, inspects the progress of work during the rebuilding of her city

c2000 BC
Berbers settle in Tunisia interbreeding with black Africans from south of the Sahara and blue-eyed, blond-haired immigrants from the north.

1100 BC
Phoenician traders establish trading posts along Tunisia's Mediterranean coastline including Sousse, Bizerte and Utica.

814 BC
The Phoenicians build the walled city of Carthage and rule a vast commercial empire for the next seven centuries.

146 BC
A long and violent struggle ends with the destruction of Carthage by the Romans.

44 BC
After defeating Pompey at the battle of Thapsus near Mahdia, Julius Caesar rebuilds Carthage. Over the next 400 years it becomes a major administrative centre and the third largest city of the Roman Empire.

AD 423
Carthage is destroyed by the Vandals, a Germanic tribe which has already pillaged its way through France and Spain, desecrating religious images.

533
Byzantines restore the port of Carthage and create a series of massive fortresses and magnificent churches.

647
Following the death of the Prophet Mohammed in 632, Arab armies arrive from the east killing the Byzantine Prefect Gregory at Sbeitla in 647 and imposing Islam on the population.

797
Ibrahim ibn al Aghlab puts down a revolt and founds a dynasty. The Aghlabids build the Grande Mosquée de Sidi Oqba at Kairouan and the Grande Mosquée at Sousse, and introduce a sophisticated irrigation system, planting thousands of citrus trees.

909–1229
The Fatmids, Zirids, Almohads and Almoravids take turns at control.

1230–1574
The Hafsids make Tunis the capital and establish

international trade in gold, ostrich feathers, ebony, ivory and precious oils during a relatively long period of stability. This is followed by a century of gradual decline.

1574
After a long power struggle between the Ottoman Turks and Spanish Hapsburgs Tunis comes under the control of the Ottoman Empire which appoints a ruling *pasha* who, relies on a network of local *beys* (provincial governors) to enforce laws and collect taxes.

1704–1881
Hussein ibn Ali Turki takes control. Under the Husaynids the economy prospers as the *beys* exercise their monopoly to generate a vibrant trade in agricultural products.

1878
The Ottoman Empire is divided up at the Congress of Berlin and France announces it has a claim on Tunisia. Three years later it invades the country and in 1883 declares Tunisia a French protectorate.

1934
Radical lawyer Habib Bourguiba (► 14) forms the Neo-Destour Party.

1938
Anti-French demonstrators are killed by troops in Tunis. Bourguiba is arrested and imprisoned in France.

1956
Tunisia gains independence from France and a year later declares itself a republic with Habib Bourguiba as its first president.

1987
President Bourguiba is removed from office by his prime minister, the former army general Zine el-Abidine Ben Ali.

1988
Tunisia forms the Union du Grand Maghreb (Arab Maghreb Union) with Morocco, Algeria, Libya and Mauritania to help counter the impact of the European Union.

1991
President Ben Ali condemns the Iraqi invasion of Kuwait, but does not send troops to join the US-led Desert Shield force against Iraq.

1995
Tunisia signs an association agreement with the European Union which will lead to free trade with the EU after 12 years.

Habib Bourguiba, depicted with his dog, is commemorated by this statue in the public gardens in central Tabarka

Peace & Quiet

It is easy to get away from it all in Tunisia, since there is only one major city and much of the rest of the country is sparsely populated. The country has only a handful of national parks and municipal gardens, but there are few restrictions on wandering in the countryside.

The Coastline

The Roman historian Pliny the Elder (AD 23–79) described the Tunisian coastline as being one of the finest in the world, and nearly 2,000 years later he would probably still hold the same view. Tourist resorts have developed along some of the finest stretches of beach, but with more than 1,100km of coastline available, much of the rest remains completely unspoilt.

Quieter beaches include Raf Raf Plage, a glorious crescent-shaped stretch of fine white sand 38km east of Bizerte facing the small rocky island of Pilau, which is good for snorkelling and underwater fishing. The beach is partly bordered by the small village of Raf Raf and by dunes and pinewoods. Near by is the isolated beach of Sidi Ali el Mekki, where a small number of cafés and a few straw huts for camping are the only facilities. To the west of Bizerte, Rass Engelah is overlooked by a picturesque Moorish lighthouse.

The area around Tabarka has been dubbed the 'Coral Coast' (➤ 43) and the waters are so crystal clear that it offers excellent diving.

The beach at Raf Raf is popular with day trippers from Bizerte and Tunis

The Desert

Wind-furrowed sand dunes near Douz

The Sahara Desert covers nearly the whole of southern Tunisia and the popular image of shifting sands sweeping across a relentlessly barren landscape is an accurate description of the landscape found in the Grand Erg Oriental. Only suitable for four-wheel-drive vehicles and then only when accompanied by skilled drivers and guides, most holidaymakers are content to experience a less harsh version of the desert.

This can be found in the area around Tunisia's two great *chotts* (salt lakes), Chott el Jerid (➤ 82) and Chott el Gharsa (➤ 87), which sit below sea level and are fringed by beautiful oases. Only a few kilometres outside the main desert centres of Nefta (➤ 85) and Tozeur (➤ 87) one can be driving on a totally empty road. Get out and walk around and the silence is almost deafening. Douz (➤ 83) is one of the best places to go for a camel ride into the desert.

DID YOU KNOW?

Arabs have more than a hundred different words to describe a camel. A familiar sight in the southern half of the country, the so-called 'ship of the desert' is an extraordinary animal which can survive for months without water and when it does finally get the chance for a drink it can consume up to 130 litres in one go. Talk about quenching your thirst!

Flora and Fauna

Tunisia was once home to an exotic array of wildlife, including lions and elephants, which has long since disappeared. Today the largest animal existing in any number is the wild boar which is found in the forests around Tabarka (➤ 43) where there are also jackals, porcupines and mongooses. Wild animals in the desert region include foxes, snakes, horned vipers and scorpions – so it is best not to walk around barefoot!

More than two hundred different species of bird have been recorded in Tunisia. Jebel Ichkeul National Park (➤ 19, Top Ten) is a stopping-off point in the spring and autumn migration seasons between Europe and Africa.

Prickly pears are known here as Barbary figs

Tunisia's Famous

Below: *Habib Bourguiba strove for independence from French rule, and instituted education for all*

Habib Bourguiba (1903–)

Habib Bourguiba became the republic's first president and is widely known as the father of modern Tunisia. He was born in Monastir in 1903 and educated at the elite Sadiki College in Tunis, and in Paris where he studied law. Bourguiba's political career did not begin until 1932 when, back in Tunis, he started a newspaper, *L'Action Tunisienne*. Two years later he founded the populist Neo-Destour Party which was committed to independence from France. Six months after its foundation the party was declared illegal and for the first of many times over the next two decades Bourguiba was arrested and imprisoned.

Immediately after World War II Bourguiba travelled to many world capitals highlighting Tunisia's plight, gaining considerable support. In 1955 he accepted a French plan for an autonomous state and on 20 March 1956 the country gained independence. The following year the new republic was established and Bourguiba became its first president. He governed for 31 years, until removed from office by the current president Zine el-Abidine Ben Ali. He was sometimes criticised for his autocratic style but his achievements included forging a strong national identity, providing for universal education and elevating the role of women in Tunisian society.

Ibn Khaldun (1332–1406)
Ibn Khaldun, the Tunis-born philosopher and politician, spent four years writing a massive volume on North African history but made a greater impact with *Muqaddima*, a brief introduction to the history of the world. Khaldun is thought to be the first person to write about cyclical patterns in history and the nature and levelopment of society, ich now form some of the principles of modern-iology.

Hannibal (247–182 BC)

Hannibal, although born in Spain, is considered an honorary Tunisian as his birth took place on Carthaginian territory. His most famous exploit occurred during the second Punic war when he invaded Italy from the north after crossing the Alps with an army of 40,000 men and 300 elephants. Support from Carthage collapsed just as Rome seemed to be within his grasp and he was recalled home. In 202 BC Hannibal was defeated by the Roman general Scipio Africanus at the battle of Zama near Le Kef. Forced into exile in Syria and later to (what is now) Turkey, he committed suicide by poison to avoid capture by the Romans.

Top Ten

Dougga 16
El Jem 17
Iles Kerkennah 18
Jebel Ichkeul National Park 19
Kairouan 20–1
Ksar Ouled Soltane 22
Musée du Bardo, Tunis 23
Qasr el-Aïn, Nefta 24
Sidi Bou Saïd 25
Thermes d'Antonin (Antonine Baths) 26

Above: *parts of Ksar Ouled Soltane are over 400 years old*
Right: *Tunisia's most famous mosaic depicts Virgil, Clio and Melpomene*

1
Dougga

28B5

110km southwest of Tunis

Daily 7–7 (8:30–5:30 in winter)

Small café (£) near the entrance serving drinks and light snacks in summer, drinks only in winter

Hourly daytime services from Tunis to Le Kef which stop at Nouvelle Dougga 3km from the site. Difficult to reach the site without a car. Taxis available from Tebersouk

Cheap

Summer plays and concerts in Dougga's theatre. Times and dates variable

Dougga is a splendid monument to Roman precision building, with many columns still standing

Tunisia's best-preserved and most spectacular Roman ruins have a dramatic setting on a hillside with wide views of the surrounding countryside.

The Roman town of Dougga was built on the site of the ancient settlement of Thugga, which had become the seat of the Numidian king Massinissa in the 2nd century BC. Dougga prospered under Roman rule and at its peak is thought to have had a population of between 5,000 and 10,000 people. In the early 1950s residents were moved to the nearby purpose-built village of Nouvelle Dougga.

Fervent archaeologists will find Dougga worth a full day's visit, and even those with a limited interest need to allow at least two hours just to see the main buildings. It is advisable – particularly in summer – to arrive as early as possible to avoid the crowds and intense midday heat.

Dougga's star attraction is the well-preserved Capitol built in AD 166 and dedicated to Jupiter, Juno and Minerva. The Roman Theatre, cut into the hillside, is the most complete of any in Tunisia and is still used by a summer touring company. There is a magnificent view over the surrounding wheat fields and olive groves from the impressive Temple of Saturn, dedicated to the sun god Baal Hammon. The centrepiece of the nearby Plaza of the Winds is a compass-like wind-indicator inscribed with the names of the 12 Roman winds. The house of Trifolium is thought to have been the town's brothel; the latrines immediately beside it suggest that this most private of functions was a sociable experience – a dozen seats are set in a horseshoe-shaped row.

2
El Jem

The amphitheatre at El Jem is one of the Roman Empire's greatest legacies to Tunisia.

El Jem is only slightly smaller than the Colosseum in Rome, but it is better preserved and much more imposing, though situated incongruously at the end of a street of modern houses. If it were near a major European holiday destination there is little doubt it would be packed solid with visitors year-round, so try to see it soon before the crowds get there. Early morning is good for taking photographs and dusk is particularly atmospheric.

There is very open access; a few areas have been roped off but only to protect visitors from dangerous drops. Pleasingly, there are no signs or notices inside the amphitheatre, making it easier to imagine the colourful festivals or the bloody dawn-to-dusk gladiatorial contests that were held here. The gladiators – often simply petty thieves, debtors or prisoners – would be pitted against each other or against wild animals to fight to the death.

Built between AD 230 and 238 in the busy market town of Thysdrus, the amphitheatre could seat crowds of more than 30,000. Measuring 149m long by 124m wide, even today it would be considered an impressive building achievement but without modern equipment it is an awesome feat of engineering. In the absence of suitable materials locally, blocks of sandstone were transported from quarries 30km away while water was carried 15km through an underground aqueduct.

El Jem archaeological museum has some attractive 3rd-century mosaics on display.

28C5

70km south of Sousse

Daily 7–7 (8–5 in winter)

Café (£) directly opposite entrance to the amphitheatre

On the main line south to Sfax and north to Sousse and Tunis

None

Moderate

International Festival of Symphonic Music in July

Archaeological Museum

1km south of the amphitheatre on the road to Sfax

7–7 (8–5 in winter)

Included in price of ticket to amphitheatre

The Roman amphitheatre at El Jem could hold 30,000

3
Iles Kerkennah

A watchtower built in the 16th century for surveying the islands

The cluster of seven islands 20km off the coast of Sfax has been called 'The Last Paradise' and would appeal to anyone trying to get away from it all.

28C4

20km east of Sfax

La Sirène (££) on the beachfront in Remla (► 96)

Regular ferry services to Sfax from Sidi Youssef. The journey takes about an hour with at least four services a day in winter and departures every two hours in summer

Buses meet all ferries and all stop in Remla

None

Once a place of exile for the Carthaginian general Hannibal and Tunisia's former president Habib Bourguiba (► 14), there are two main inhabited islands, Chergui and Gharbi, joined together by a causeway. The islands are reached by ferry from Sfax, arriving at Sidi Youssef on the south-western tip of the islands, with a single main road running 35km north to the fishing village of El Attaia.

Fishing remains the main source of income for most of the 15,000 islanders. Strings of clay pots for catching squid can be seen on many quaysides; palm fronds are used to channel fish into waiting nets. Although tourism now supplements the islands' economy it remains very low-key and recent plans by the Tunisian government to transform Iles Kerkennah into a massive purpose-built resort area appear to have been dropped. The small west coast tourist zone of Sidi Frej consists of a handful of modest hotels.

Borj el-Hissar, an old fort 3km north of Sidi Frej, was built by the Spanish in the 16th century; it is surrounded by Roman ruins and has the remains of several mosaics. Remla, the biggest settlement, has a few shops and cafés and one hotel, the Jazira (► 104). With its shallow waters and long stretches of empty sandy beaches, the area is well-suited to walking and cycling.

4
Jebel Ichkeul National Park

One of only two wetland conservation areas to be designated World Heritage Sites by UNESCO (the other is the Everglades in Florida).

Telescopes enable visitors to view the birdlife of Lake Ichkeul

Jebel Ichkeul is the most important bird sanctuary in North Africa and provides a vital stopping point for birds migrating between Europe and Africa. If you visit at dawn or dusk from October to February, thousands of waterfowl can be spotted on the lake.

Rarer birds on the lake include the marbled teal and the purple gallinule, one of Tunisia's most colourful birds. Looking rather like an oversized moorhen, it has a bright red beak and gleaming purple-blue plumage. Sandpipers, stints and stilts are regularly found on the shores of Lac d'Ichkeul and Moussier's redstarts which are indigenous to North Africa can be spotted in the scrub. The park is also home to many animals including water buffalo, wild boar, jackals, otters and porcupines.

The park is a tranquil and uplifting place to visit at any time of the year; there are some picnic tables and several walking trails. Poppies and wild chrysanthemums bloom in the fields around the lake, and from the car park a steep climb leads to a small **Eco-Museum** which details the area's flora and fauna and explains the ecological importance of the lake. It also has a collection of stuffed birds.

There is nowhere to stay in the park and camping is not permitted, but it is easily accessible from Tunis.

28B6

30km southwest of Bizerte

Daily 7–6

Bring your own picnic, tables provided

No public transport; hire car essential

None

Inexpensive

Eco-Museum

9–12, 1:30–4:30

None

Cheap

5
Kairouan

28B5

70km west of Sousse

Sabra (£), avenue de la République – good value set menus. Fairouz (£–££) just north of the *souqs* on rue des Tailleurs – worth paying extra for

Bus station on the main route between Tunis and the south

Place des Bassins des Aglabides ☎ 07 231 897 Sat–Thu 8–6, Fri 8–1. Multiple entry ticket provides access to most of the city's major attractions

Mouled Festival to celebrate the Prophet Muhammad's birthday, June

Grande Mosquée de Sidi Oqba

Boulevard Ibrahim ibn Aghlab (main gate on Boulevard Brahim ben Lagheb)

7:30–2 (8–2:30 in winter). Closes noon on Fri

Cheap

None

Opposite: *the minaret and colonnades of the Great Mosque*
Right: *footwear is removed before entering the prayer hall of the Zaouia de Sidi Sahab*

Kairouan is Tunisia's holiest city, with more than 50 mosques within the médina.

Kairouan is the fourth most important city in the Islamic world after Mecca, Médina and Jerusalem. The **Grande Mosquée de Sidi Oqba** (Great Mosque) is the star attraction here; the existing building was constructed by the Aghlabids in AD 863. Non-Muslims are forbidden to enter the prayer hall with its 400 marble pillars, many of which were recovered from the ruins of Carthage and El Jem, but visitors may be allowed to take a look through one of the 17 heavy cedar wood doors at one of the world's oldest pulpits decorated with 250 carved wood panels. Entry may also be permitted to the 128-step staircase – made from Christian tombstones – to the top of the square minaret for a superb panorama of the city.

The Mosquée des Trois Portes (Mosque of the Three Doors) also dates from the 9th century and features three arched doorways providing separate entrances for men, women and children.

The Zaouia de Sidi Sahab (Shrine of the Companion) on avenue de la République is the burial place of Abou Zamaa el-Balaoui, a friend of the Prophet. It is sometimes known as the Barber's Mosque as el-Balaoui always wore a medallion containing three hairs from the Prophet's beard. The original mausoleum dates back to the 7th century but tiled archways, antechambers and beautiful floral mosaics were added at the end of the 17th century.

The Bassins des Aglabides (Aghlabid Pools), ten minutes' walk to the east, were part of an elaborate 9th century water system which collected rain from the Tell Plateau via a 35km aqueduct.

6
Ksar Ouled Soltane

28C3

22km east of Tataouine

All day

Hôtel les Ghorfas (£), 6km west of Metameur; Hôtel Ksar Hadada (£)

Three buses a day from Tataouine

Free

Ksar Hallouf (☎ 05 647037). Ruins of 12th-century *ksar* 8km west

The exterior steps of the ksour *look less than safe*

One of the enduring legacies of the Berber culture, ksour *originally served as fortified grain stores.*

Built from mud and stone, *ksour* (singular '*ksar*') are a familiar sight in southern Tunisia especially around Tataouine. In the hostile desert climate there might only be a good crop once every few years making it essential to defend supplies from attack by other tribes. Cool conditions inside the *ksour's* claustrophobic, barrel-vaulted rooms (known as *ghorfas*) meant that grain could be kept for several years without deteriorating. It was typical for *ksour* to be clustered together around a courtyard and to be linked by internal steps and passageways. Usually three or four stories high, some of the *ksour* at Ouled Soltane have precarious-looking outside steps.

The earliest surviving *ksour* are up to 800 years old but Ksar Ouled Soltane is among the best-known because it is particularly well preserved. Buildings in the first courtyard are more than 400 years old while the second complex dates from around 1850. Situated some way off the beaten track – nearly a three-hour drive from Jerba – like many of Tunisia's most impressive sights it remains largely undiscovered by tourists and it is not unusual to find you are the only visitor. One of the most rewarding times to visit is on Friday afternoons, when the courtyard becomes a meeting point for the local community.

A visit to Ouled Soltane is often combined with trips to other *ksour* in the area including the 13th-century Ksar Hallouf near Zammour, part of which has been converted into a very simple hotel with primitive toilet facilities. Better quality accommodation and lunches are available at the *ksour* in Metameur, 6km west of Medenine, and also at Ksar Haddada.

7
Musée du Bardo, Tunis

Tunisia's national museum houses archaeological treasures from all over the country but is known principally for its impressive collection of mosaics.

The Musée du Bardo is housed in a former palace of the Husaynid *beys* (provincial governors). It is arranged in sections covering the Carthaginian, Roman, early Christian and Islamic eras. The undoubted highlight is the Roman section, where entire walls and floors are paved with mosaics from the 2nd century BC to the 7th century AD, many almost intact. The 3rd-century mosaic of the poet Virgil writing the *Aeneid* attended by two muses, found in a villa in Sousse (➤ 60), and the giant Triumph of Neptune mosaic are among the most exceptional exhibits. Another captivating 3rd-century work which was found at Dougga (➤ 16, Top Ten) is the mosaic of Ulysses and his sailors resisting the songs of three sirens trying to lure their vessel on to the rocks. The mosaic of Perseus rescuing Andromeda from the clutches of a sea monster was taken from an underground villa at Bulla Regia (➤ 42). Many of the smaller mosaics feature common themes including hunting and farming scenes, Greek and Roman gods, the sea, battles and family life. Animals, birds and fish are also widely depicted. Apart from the mosaics there are dozens of statues, stelae and sarcophagi from the Carthaginian and Roman periods, including a priceless terracotta statue of the sun god Baal Hammon sitting on a throne and wearing a feathered head-dress. There is also a spectacular collection of bronze and marble figures, which were recovered from the wreck of a ship which came to grief off the coast of Mahdia in the first century BC.

32A2 (arrowed)

Route de Bizerte, Quartier Le Bardo, 6km from city centre

01 513842, Fax 01 514050.

Tue–Sun 9–6; 9:30–4:30 in winter. Closed Mon

Small café on ground floor (£)

Line 4 from Tunis city centre

3 from avenue Habib Bourguiba

Few

Moderate

Above left: *the* Triumph of Neptune *mosaic*
Above: *the magnificent decorated doorway to the Musée du Bardo*

8
Qasr el-Aïn, Nefta

28A4

Avenue des Sources

All day

Drinks at Café Maure el Khazen (£) and Café-Bar La Corbeille (£) which both overlook the site

Up to six buses a day from Tozeur. Also daily services from Nefta to Kairouan and Sfax

Tozeur–Nefta Airport 23km

Free

Avenue Habib Bourguiba ☎ 06 457236

Qasr el-Aïn, or the Corbeille, is the smaller of two oases in the desert town of Nefta; it is dramatically situated in a giant bowl-shaped depression.

Measuring almost 1km wide and up to 40m deep, the massive crater at Qasr el-Aïn is filled with hundreds of palm trees and is watered by 152 natural springs, many of them warm and sulphurous. The springs also supply a large bathing pool at the westerly end of the Corbeille (French for 'basket') which is very popular in summer, generally used by women and girls in the morning and men and boys in the afternoon.

The best view of the Corbeille is from a terrace directly above the bathing pool where there are a couple of cafés and no shortage of persistent but not very knowledgeable guides. It is best to hire a guide from the tourist office. Early evening is a good time to be there, when the palm grove is bathed in a warm glow. The maze of trees can be explored on foot or by donkey following several well-worn paths. Part of the area has been divided into gardens which have belonged to the same families for centuries.

The Corbeille is not quite as attractive as it once was. Some of the wells have run dry amid controversy that the town's modern tourist hotels are taking too much water for their swimming pools. Some of the palm trees have also suffered from fire and floods.

Nefta's main oasis lies in the southern part of town on the opposite side of avenue Habib Bourguiba. Covering more than 10 sq km, hundreds of thousands of palm trees here are watered by 200 springs.

Bunches of ripening fruit hang from a date palm in the Corbeille

9
Sidi Bou Saïd

Sidi Bou Saïd is invariably described as Tunisia's prettiest village and is almost a compulsory stop on any excursion from Tunisia's beach resorts.

Sidi Bou Saïd somehow manages to avoid being a total tourist trap and a blatant distortion of a real Tunisian village. It retains considerable charm and beauty and is always a pleasant place to while away a few of hours. Situated northeast of Tunis and connected by regular metro services, the hilltop village is known for its cobbled streets and whitewashed houses with blue window grilles and studded doors. Its focal point is the main square, place Sidi Bou Saïd, which is lined with cafés and souvenir shops.

The village's history goes back to the 9th century when a fortified monastery was built here as part of a chain of coastal defences aimed at deterring Christian invaders. In the 13th century a community began to form around the tomb of a holy man – Sidi Bou Saïd – whose life is still celebrated during a festival each August. In the late 19th century wealthy French expatriates began buying houses in the village. In 1912 an English baron with the unlikely name of Rodolphe d'Erlanger spent ten years building an exquisite cliffside villa and gardens here – Ennejma Ezzahra. Laws were passed to protect the village and to order that the only colours that could be used in external decoration would be the now ubiquitous bright blue and white. D'Erlanger's palatial home has become Le Centre des Musiques Arabes et Mediterranéennes (Centre for Arab and Mediterranean Music) where concerts are held and there is a fascinating collection of musical instruments.

28B6

20km northeast of Tunis.

Mint tea and coffee at Café des Nattes (£) and Café Sidi Chabanne (£) (► 92)

TGM metro services from Tunis every 20 mins. Journey time 30 mins. 15 min uphill walk from the station to the centre of the village

None

Celebration of the life of Sidi Bou Saïd in August

Le Centre des Musiques Arabes et Mediterranéennes

Ennejma Ezzahra

Tue–Sun, 9–12, 2–7 (2–5 only in winter). Closed Mon

Concerts in July and December

Blue doors, flowers and dazzling white walls in Sidi Bou Saïd

10
Thermes d'Antonin (Antonine Baths)

Once the biggest Roman baths in the Empire and Carthage's best-preserved site.

37C2

Avenue des Thermes d'Antonin

Daily 8–7 (8:30–5:30 in winter). Closed on public holidays

Drinks at Café des Nattes or Café Sidi Chabanne, Sidi Bou Saïd (► 92)

Regular TGM metro services from Tunis to Carthage–Hannibal station

None

Cheap (ticket will also provide entry to other Carthage ruins and the Musée National de Carthage)

Above: *a section of the great bathhouse complex*

The site is entered from the top of a colourful garden which slopes gently down to the sea following the pattern of the original Roman streets. Close to the entrance are the remains of a *schola* which was a kind of after-school boys' club for the sons of wealthy Romans, with an unusual mosaic showing children doing physical exercises. The ruins of the Byzantine Basilica of Douimes are marked by three rows of double pillars and a mosaic floor.

Visitors are not allowed to enter the baths, but can study them from a viewing platform. A white marble model shows what the baths would have been like when they were in daily use and a couple of pillars have been repositioned to give an idea of the original height.

Work on the baths began during the reign of the Roman Emperor Hadrian (AD 76–138) who spent a considerable amount of time touring his vast empire and promoting urban life. When the baths were completed, under Antoninus Pius, they were the largest outside Rome. Heat was provided by an underground system of furnaces and there was a series of hot rooms of varying temperatures, a cold plunge pool and a Roman 'whirlpool', (without the bubbles of course).

The baths are surrounded by an archaeological park with a number of Punic tombs, and the site borders the presidential palace, the official residence of the Tunisian leader, President Ben Ali.

What to See

Tunis and the North	29–45
Cap Bon	47–55
Food and Drink	56–7
Central Tunisia	59–73
In the Know	74–5
Jerba and the South	77–90

Above: *scarlet national flags of Tunisia outside the Palais du Congrès*
Right: *an Arab horseman at the Festival of the Sahara, Douz*

TUNISIA
La Galite
Bizerte
Cap Blanc
Parc National de Jebel Ichkeul
Tinja
Utica
Ghar el Melh
Sidi Mechrig
Mateur
Menzel Bourguiba
Cap Bon
El Haouaria
Kerkouane
Kelibia
Tabarka
Gammarth
La Marsa
Sidi Bou Said
Korbous
Carthage
La Goulette
Aïn Draham
Béja
Mejez El Bab
Mejerda
TUNIS
Menze Temime
Thuburnica
Bou Salem
Bulla Regia
Jendouba
Testour
Korba
Téboursouk
Dougga
Monts de Téboursouk
Thuburbo Majus
Zaghouan
Nabeul
Hammamet
El Fahs
Le Kef
Enfida
Hergla
Port el Kantaoui
Dorsale
Makthar
Kairouan
Sousse
Skanès
Monastir
Sabel
Thala
Tell
Moknine
Mahdia
Ruines de Sbeïtla
Kasserine
Sbeïtla
El Jem
Ksour Essaf
1544 m Jebel Chambi
Rass Kaboudia
Sidi Bouzid
Sfax
Meknassy
Sabel
Iles Kerkennah
Midès
Tamerza
Gorges de Selja
Gafsa
El Guettar
Mahrès
Chebika
Metlaoui
Golfe de Gabès
Chott el Gharsa
Nefta
Degache
Tozeur
Chott el Fejaj
Houmt-Souk
Gabès
Midoun
Qasr el-Ain
Chott el Jerid
Erriadh
Ile de Jerba
Ajim
El Kantara
Guellala
Kebili
Matmata
Monts des Ksour
Metameur
Zarzis
Douz
Medenine
Ksar Hallouf
Ksar Haddada
Ghomrassen
Foum Tataouine
Ben Gardane
Ksar Ghilane
Chenini
Dahar
Ksar Ouled Soltane
Grand Erg Oriental
Remada
Dehibat
DZ
L-R
Borj el Khadra
0
50
100
150 km
A
B
C
1
2
3
4
5
6

Tunis & the North

Although northern Tunisia is home to nearly a quarter of the population, thousands of holiday-makers bypass this area altogether and head straight for the east coast beach resorts. This is a pity as the capital is here and the surrounding countryside and coastline are enormously varied.

Tunis has more than enough attractions to warrant a few nights' stay or, at the very least, a full day's excursion. For more than 3,000 years, Tunis has been among the great cities of the Mediterranean and it still has plenty to offer. It would also provide a convenient base for independent travellers, with dozens of quiet beaches and some of the country's finest archaeological sites within easy reach.

Tabarka is emerging as Tunisia's northern flagship resort, while the charming old port town of Bizerte is still debating whether it really wants to entice international tourists or is quite content to remain a sleepy backwater.

'Around Carthage, immobile waves glistened as the moon spread its beams on the gulf surrounded by mountains and on the Lake of Tunis.'

GUSTAVE FLAUBERT,
1821–80

Tunis

28B6
66km southeast of Bizerte, 120km northwest of Sousse
1 avenue Moham V 01 341077 8:30–1, 3–5.45 Mon–Thu, 8:30–1:30 Fri, Sat

Tunis started life as a small garrison town, defended by the high walls of its *médina*. Its expansion into a wealthy trading city was sparked by the Arab invasion of Tunisia in the 7th century, though it was another 600 years before Tunis became the capital.

Today the city is the undisputed focal point of the nation. It is home to one in ten of the population and forms the epicentre of political, cultural and social life. The city combines a vibrant, atmospheric old town of narrow lanes and covered *souqs* with the more European-style Ville Nouvelle characterised by tree-lined avenues and elegant colonnaded, balconied buildings.

What to See in Tunis

AVENUE HABIB BOURGUIBA

33C2
Café at L'Africa Méridien (£) (▶ 101), 50 avenue Habib Bourguiba; Le Baghdad (££–£££) (▶ 92)
5, 8, 35, 50
Line 1, Tunis Marine

The 'Champs Elysées' of Tunis, avenue Habib Bourguiba is the capital's best-known and most prestigious thoroughfare, but like its more famous sister it is not quite as elegant as one might have imagined. Apart from a few grand buildings there is a mishmash of banks, *bureaux de change*, *pâtisseries*, cinemas, car rental agents and hotels, including L'Africa Méridien – the street's most prominent landmark and a popular meeting place (▶ 101).

Avenue Habib Bourguiba begins at the foot of avenue de France close to the main entrance to the *médina*. Where the streets run together is the **Cathédrale de St Vincente de Paul**, a Catholic church built in 1882. Just across the road is the Ambassade de France (French Embassy) from where the Protectorate was governed between 1881 and the granting of independence in 1956. Further east is the art nouveau-style Theatre Municipal which has recently been refurbished and is regularly used for concerts.

Cathédrale de St Vincente de Paul
33C2
Avenue Habib Bourguiba
8.30–11.30, 3–6PM. Daily service at 6.30PM and Sundays at 9 and 11AM
Free (donations accepted)

Above: the Avenue imparts something of a French air to the city

JEMAA EZ ZITOUNA ✪✪

Jemaa ez Zitouna (the Great Mosque) covers an area of more than 5,000 sq m and is the largest mosque in Tunis, dwarfing the surrounding alleyways. It has been at the spiritual heart of Tunis for over 1,000 years and is the only mosque in the city which can be visited by non-Muslims, though access is restricted to a viewing enclosure overlooking the polished marble courtyard.

Jemaa ez Zitouna (literally Mosque of the Olive Tree) dates mostly from the middle of the 9th century, though it has been modified many times since, and was inspired by the slightly larger Grande Mosquée de Sidi Oqba (Great Mosque) in Kairouan (➤ 20, Top Ten). Its outer wall is built of stone taken from Roman Carthage. The courtyard is flanked on three sides by simple arcades and on the fourth by a prayer hall supported by 184 columns.

During the 13th and 14th centuries the mosque became an important Islamic university attracting students from all over the Arab world. It continued to flourish until the 1950s when the teaching faculty was closed on the orders of President Bourguiba in a bid to reduce religious influence in the country. The mosque and its 500-year-old library, containing one of the world's greatest collections of Arab literature, had its teaching status restored by in 1987 by President Ben Ali.

- 32B2
- Rue Jemaa ez Zitouna
- 8AM–12. Closed Fri
- Café ez Zitouna (£), rue Jemaa ez Zitouna
- 1
- Habib Thameur
- None
- Cheap

The square minaret of Jemaa ez Zitouna can be seen from rooftop terraces in the souq

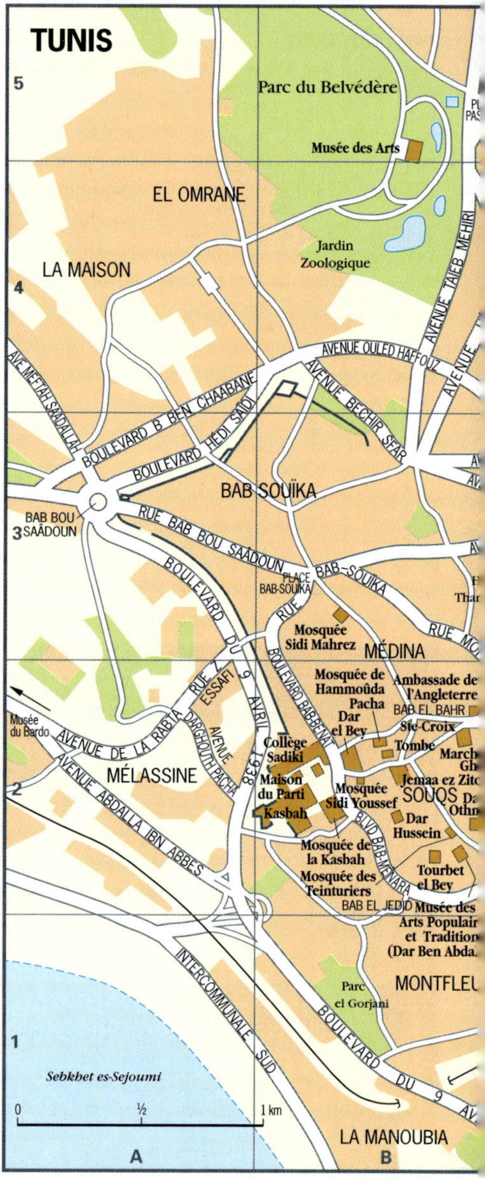
TUNIS
5
Parc du Belvédère
Musée des Arts
EL OMRANE
Jardin
Zoologique
LA MAISON
4
AVENUE TAIEB MEHIRI
AVENUE OULED HAFFOUZ
AVE MEFTAH SAADALLAH
BOULEVARD B BEN CHAABANE
BOULEVARD HÉDI SAIDI
AVENUE BECHIR SFAR
BAB SOUÏKA
BAB BOU
3 SAÂDOUN
RUE BAB BOU SAÂDOUN
PLACE
BAB-SOUIKA
BAB-SOUIKA
BOULEVARD DU 9 AVRIL 1938
RUE
Mosquée
Sidi Mahrez
MÉDINA
BOULEVARD BAB-BENAT
Mosquée de
Hammoûda
Pacha
Ambassade de
l'Angleterre
BAB EL BAHR
Dar
el Bey
Ste-Croix
Tombe
RUE ZESSAFI
Musée
du Bardo
AVENUE DE LA RABTA
AVENUE DARGHOUTH PACHA
Collège
Sadiki
Maison
du Parti
Kasbah
MÉLASSINE
Mosquée
Sidi Youssef
SOUQS
Jemaa ez Zitouna
2
AVENUE ABDALLA IBN ABBES
BLVD BAB-MENARA
Dar
Hussein
Mosquée de
la Kasbah
Mosquée des
Teinturiers
Tourbet
el Bey
BAB EL JEDID
Musée des
Arts Populaires
et Traditions
(Dar Ben Abdallah)
INTERCOMMUNALE SUD
Parc
el Gorjani
MONTFLEURY
1
BOULEVARD DU 9 AVRIL
Sebkhet es-Sejoumi
0
½
1 km
LA MANOUBIA
A
B

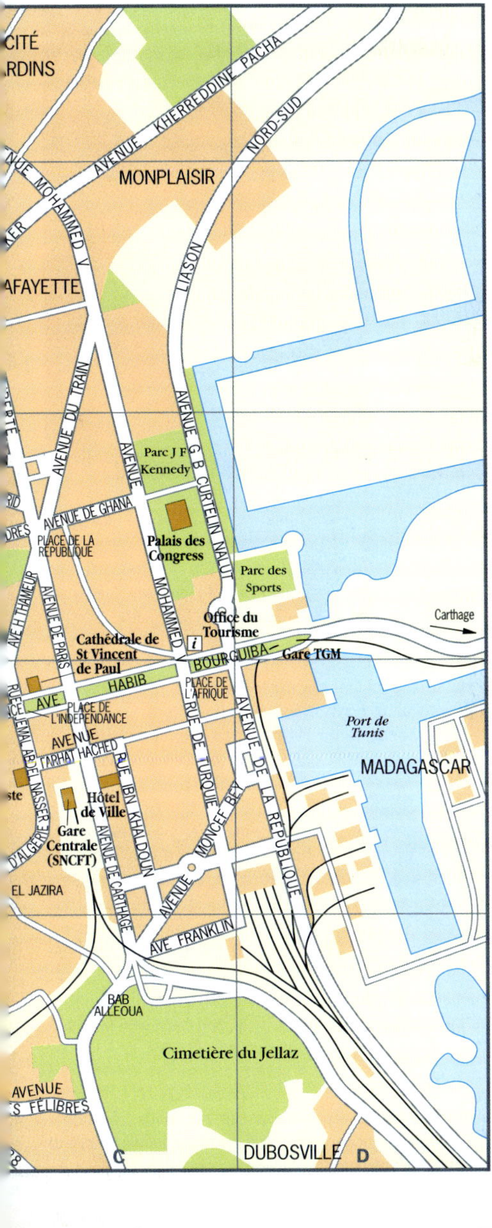
CITÉ
RDINS
AVENUE KHERREDDINE PACHA
NORD-SUD
MONPLAISIR
AVENUE MOHAMMED V
LIASON
AFAYETTE
AVENUE DU TRAIN
AVENUE G B CURTELIN NALUT
AVENUE
Parc J F Kennedy
AVENUE DE GHANA
PLACE DE LA RÉPUBLIQUE
Palais des Congress
Parc des Sports
AVE H THAMEUR
AVENUE DE PARIS
MOHAMMED
Office du Tourisme
Carthage
Cathédrale de St Vincent de Paul
BOURGUIBA
Gare TGM
HABIB
AVE
PLACE DE L'AFRIQUE
PLACE DE L'INDÉPENDANCE
RUE DE TURQUIE
AVENUE DE LA RÉPUBLIQUE
Port de Tunis
AVENUE TARHAT HACHED
RUE JEMAL ABDEL NASSER
MADAGASCAR
RUE IBN KHALDOUN
AVENUE MONCEF BEY
Hôtel de Ville
Gare Centrale (SNCFT)
AVENUE DE CARTHAGE
EL JAZIRA
AVE FRANKLIN
BAB ALLEOUA
Cimetière du Jellaz
AVENUE
S FÉLIBRES
C
DUBOSVILLE
D

Right: *sacks of spices and bundles of dried herbs give a particular scent to the* souq

Bab el Bahr
32B3
Place de la Victoire
1
Habib Thameur
Plenty of choice
Difficult

Mosquée de Hammoûda Pacha
32B2

Mosquée Sidi Youssef
32B2

Dar Othman
32B2

Tourbet el Bey
32B2

MÉDINA ✪✪✪

The medieval part of Tunis is listed by UNESCO as a World Heritage Site. It dates back to the 7th century and remained the commercial centre of the city until the establishment of the French Protectorate in 1881, after which it began to decline. Start by exploring the narrow alleys at the **Bab el Bahr** (also known as the Sea Gate or Porte de France) on place de la Victoire. The arched gateway passes through the old city wall and dates from 1848.

The **Mosquée de Hammoûda Pacha** with its thin Turkish-style minaret, built in 1655 to honour an Italian who had converted to Islam, and the **Mosquée Sidi Youssef** with an octagonal minaret, the oldest of its type in the city, are closed to non-Muslims. There is a good view of Sidi Youssef from the rooftop of the Musée des Turcs, an antique shop in the Souq et-Trouk. **Dar Othman** was a palace built for Othman Dey, who ruled Tunisia from 1598 to 1610, and has a pretty courtyard garden with cypress and lemon trees. The rue des Libraires contains three small 18th-century *medresa* (theological schools) at numbers 11, 27 and on the corner of the street. **Tourbet el Bey** in rue Tourbet el Bey is a royal mausoleum built in the late 18th century for the Husaynid princes.

A stroll around the northern part of the *médina* will reveal the small community which still lives here much as it has for centuries. Narrow streets, with traditional wooden, nail-studded doors and grilled windows, seem to keep their secrets to themselves.

MUSÉE DES ARTS POPULAIRES ET TRADITIONS ✪✪

The Museum of Popular Arts and Traditions occupies a late 18th-century palace, the Dar Ben Abdallah. The ornate entrance leads into a marble courtyard with a fountain, showing the visitor a tantalising example of the largely hidden side of the old city. In many ways the building itself is more interesting than the exhibition rooms which show upper class urban life in Tunis in the 19th century.

- 32B2
- Impasse Ben Abdallah, off rue Sidi Kacem
- 01 256195
- Tue–Sun 9:30–4:30
- Plenty of choice
- 1
- Habib Thameur
- None
- Moderate

MUSÉE DU BARDO (➤ 22, TOP TEN)

PARC DU BELVÉDÈRE ✪

The Belvedere Park was laid out by the French as an exclusive enclave for the families of the ruling classes. Today, with so few green open spaces in the city, the park is a popular place to escape the summer heat. An elegant 18th-century pavilion (or *koubba*) is half-way up the hill and from the top there is a good view of the city. There is also a small zoo (➤ 110).

- 32B5
- Avenue Taieb Mehiri
- Open access but avoid at night
- Couple of cafés serving drinks
- 5, 5c, 5d
- Palestine
- Free
- Concerts in summer

Zoo

- 9:00–7:00 (to 4:00 in winter)
- Café
- Cheap

Left: *traditional Tunisian woollen hats on sale in the Souq des Chechias*

SOUQS ✪✪✪

Shopping in the *souqs* (markets) is one of the biggest attractions of the *médina* for many. The myriad tiny alleys provide endless opportunities for hunting down bargains and haggling. Originally each *souq* specialised in a single trade and amongst the oldest is the 13th-century Souq el Attarine (the perfume-makers' market) which still sells scents and essential oils. The Souq des Etoffes sells fabric and clothes; search out the Souq du Cuivre (coppersmiths), the Souq des Babouches (slippers), and the Souq el-Kebabjia (silk). The Souq et-Trouk (market of the Turks) was one of the city's finest when it opened in 1630, and the Souq el-Berka was one of the largest slave markets in the Mediterranean.

- 32B2
- Throughout the *médina*
- Mostly closed on Sun
- M'Rabet Café (£), Souq et-Trouk
- 1
- Habib Thameur

28B6
15–20km northeast of Tunis
Daily 8:30–5:30 in winter, 8–7 in summer
Café des Nattes at Sidi Bou Saïd (▶ 25)
TGM every 20 mins, stopping at six stations in Carthage: Salammbo, Byrsa, Dermech, Hannibal, Presidential and Amilcar
Moderate
Carthage International Festival Jun, Jul

The elegant façade of the National Museum

Carthage

Carthage is one of the best known of Tunisia's archaeological sites, though its impact is lessened by the way the surviving treasures are scattered over a large area in a suburb of the capital.

Founded in 814 BC by the Phoenicians, by the fourth century BC Carthage had become the centre of their vast maritime empire. In 146 BC it was destroyed by the Romans who – only 25 years later – began rebuilding on the same site. It became the third largest city of the Roman Empire before it was destroyed by the Arabs in AD 692, ending its heyday.

A complete tour will take all day; it is probably less overwhelming to make a couple of shorter trips. The Musée National de Carthage (▶ right) is worth a visit for an overview of the site and to see some of the magnificent treasures, dating back to the city's earliest days.

What to See in Carthage

37A2
Carthage–Hannibal TGM station

Cathédrale de St Louis
Byrsa Hill
Concerts are held here throughout the year

BYRSA HILL ✪✪

It is possible to see the whole of the site from the summit of Byrsa Hill. This was the heart of the city under Punic rule and is the best place to start a tour. The **Cathédrale de St Louis** built here in 1890 is dedicated to the French king who died in 1279 while trying to lay siege to Tunis. The cathedral has been restored as a cultural centre for Arab music and is now known as the Acropolium.

37B4
Rue Roosevelt
Carthage–Presidential
None

CIMETIÈRE ✪

The American War Cemetery commemorates the 6,564 Americans who died in North Africa during World War II. There are 2,840 neatly tended graves and a Wall of Remembrance naming those who were never found.

LES PORTS PUNIQUES ✪

In the second century the twin Punic Ports provided berths for more than 200 naval ships but today it is almost impossible to imagine such a sight. The ports have shrunk to little more than ponds and the only way of making any sense of how they operated is to visit the small **Antiquarium** on the edge of the harbour to look at a scale model left behind by a British excavation team. It shows the ports as one giant shipyard surrounded by several slipways. The nearby **Musée Oceanographique** (Oceanographic Museum) has been modernised, with some interactive displays bringing a bit of life to an otherwise dull collection of fish and nauticalia.

37B1
Rue Hannibal
Carthage–Salammbo

Antiquarium
By the harbour
Opening times vary
Free

Musée Oceanographique
Avenue 2 Mars
01 730548
7–7. Closed Mon
Cheap

MUSÉE NATIONAL DE CARTHAGE ✪✪✪

The National Museum of Carthage houses collections of sculpture, statues, masks and mosaics. On the ground floor are Carthaginian, Roman and Christian remains, while the first-floor has incense burners and plates found inside Punic graves as well as glass, ceramics and amphorae.

37B2
01 730036
Near the cathedral
8–7 (8:30–5:30 in winter)
Dermech or Hannibal
Moderate

37B2
Daily 8–7 (8:30–5:30 in winter)
Carthage–Byrsa or Carthage–Dermech
Cheap

MUSÉE ROMAIN ET PALÉO-CHRÉTIEN ✪

The small Roman and Palaeo-Christian Museum is located at the crossroads of two ancient Roman streets over a still-intact Roman cistern. Excavations are still going on and exhibits include two peacock mosaics and a 5th-century marble statue of Ganymede.

37B2
Avenue de la République
Carthage–Hannibal
None

QUARTIER MAGON ✪

Located close to the Thermes d'Antonin (➤ 26, Top Ten), the Magon Quarter has been turned into an archaeological park. There are two small exhibition rooms and a display of mosaic pavements.

37B3
Avenue 7 Novembre
Carthage–Hannibal
None
Cheap
Carthage International Festival in the summer

THÉÂTRE D'HADRIAN ✪

There is little or nothing left of the original Theatre of Hadrian built in the early 2nd century, but it has now been completely restored and is very popular as a venue for concerts and plays during the annual Carthage International Festival. Just beyond the theatre is the Parc Archéologique des Villas Romaines (the Archaeological Park of Roman Villas), a collection of columns, statues and a few mosaics but most acknowledged for its setting with views over the Bay of Tunis.

THERMES D'ANTONIN (➤ 26, TOP TEN)

37B1
Avenue Farhat Hached
Daily 9–7 (9–5 in winter)
Carthage–Salammbo
None
Cheap

TOPHET ✪✪

It is hard to imagine this quiet, overgrown garden was used for child sacrifice. Excavations have unearthed more than 20,000 urns containing the ashes of boys aged between two and 12, sacrificed by Carthaginians in the 8th century BC. The remains were cremated as an offering to the sun god Baal Hammon and Tanit, the moon goddess.

Right: *memorial stones at Tophet serve as reminders of a cruel 8th-century ritual*

What to See Around Tunis

GAMMARTH ✪✪

Once a quiet seaside village, Gammarth is now a full-scale resort overrun with expensive hotels and restaurants. In the 1950s the beaches gained notoriety for attracting European nudists and became known locally as the Baies des Singes (Bay of Monkeys). Raoued Plage, beyond Gammarth, is a fine stretch of sand and is packed with families during the summer months.

Above the beaches, on the Hauts des Gammarth, is Jebel Khawi (Hollow Mountain), where there is a French military cemetery for more than 4,000 Frenchmen killed during World War II.

- 28B6
- 20km northeast of Tunis
- Good choice (£–£££)
- 20b from Jardin Thameur in Tunis city centre
- Few

Above: *climb Gammarth Heights for a view along the coast to Carthage*

LA GOULETTE ✪✪

Despite its rundown houses, crumbling *kasbah* and general air of neglect, La Goulette is very popular for its excellent fish restaurants attracting crowds from the city on summer weekends. Once a pirates' stronghold and home to a large Jewish community, La Goulette ('the gullet') is at the mouth of the Tunis canal and is still a major cargo and ferry port. The *kasbah*, built in 1535, was used as a dungeon for prisoners waiting to be taken to the *médina* in Tunis to be sold as slaves.

- 28B6
- 15km northeast of Tunis
- Restaurant Lucullus (£££)
  - place 7 Novembre
  - 01 737310
- TGM from Tunis Marine
- Tunis–Carthage Airport 10km. Internal flights to Jerba and Tozeur
- Few

LA MARSA ✪✪✪

La Marsa is the most upmarket beachfront suburb on the Bay of Tunis. With a palm tree-lined corniche and a long sandy beach it is a popular weekend retreat for residents of Tunis and a permanent home for the well-heeled. Two of the town's finest residences belong to the ambassadors of Britain and France.

- 28B6
- 15km northeast of Tunis
- Several (££–£££) around the metro station
- Regular TGM from Tunis
- Airport 12km
- Few

SIDI BOU SAÎD **(► 25, TOP TEN)**

The pretty French colonial church in the centre of Béja

What to See in the North

BÉJA ✪

Once among the richest and most important towns of the Maghreb, Béja has lost much of its allure and influence. Formerly a Roman garrison, the town was destroyed by the Vandals in the fifth century and again in the tenth and 11th centuries. Since then it has become an important agricultural centre.

The key attraction here is the *médina*; locally handwoven blankets are sold in Souq en-Nehasach and rue el-Attarine is the food and spice market. The Byzantine *kasbah* is used by the military and is not open to the public. There are Colonial and Commonwealth war cemeteries out beyond the station.

- 28B6
- 110km west of Tunis
- Restaurant La Belle Epoque (£), avenue de France
- Up to to seven trains a day to and from Tunis
- Frequent services from Tunis
- Few

BIZERTE ✪✪

Bizerte is the largest town on the north coast with a picturesque old port and bustling *médina*. It has only slowly begun to embrace tourism with the building of several hotels along the route de la Corniche but it is easily visited on a day trip from Tunis, less than an hour's drive away.

Bizerte has been a major port since the Phoenicians built a canal linking the inland Lac de Bizerte (Lake Bizerte) with the open sea, creating one of the finest harbours in the western Mediterranean. Known then as Hippo Zarytus, it was renamed Bizerte in 678 after being captured by the Arabs. In the 16th century – under Turkish rule – Bizerte became a pirates' den. The French made it their principal

- 28B6
- 66km northwest of Tunis
- Le Bonheur (£), 31 rue Thaalbi (➤ 92). Le Sport Nautique (£££), boulevard Habib Bougatfa (➤ 92)
- Station on rue de Rinja
- To Tunis every half-hour from Quai Tarik Ibn Zaid
- rue de Constantinople ☎ 02 432897
- Few
- Bizerte Festival Jul/Aug

naval base in the late 19th century and it has remained a military centre with young men in uniform a common sight on the town's streets.

The Vieux Port (Old Port), surrounded by shops and cafés and dotted with colourful fishing boats, is the heart of the town. At the mouth of the harbour is the ***kasbah***, which despite its Byzantine appearance dates mainly from the 17th century. In places the walls are up to 10m high and 11m thick, and within is a maze of narrow, winding passageways. Facing the *kasbah* is the smaller Sidi el-Hanni fortress, which has been turned into a small but dull **Musée Oceanographique** (Oceanographic Museum), featuring a motley collection of local fish.

West of the *kasbah* is the *médina*, which was heavily bombed during World War II. Closed to non-Muslims, the 17th-century Grande Mosquée (Great Mosque) with its octagonal minaret is best viewed from rue des Armuriers in the street behind or, better still, from the opposite side of the harbour. The **Zaouia de Sidi Mokhtar** houses the local branch of the Association de Sauvegarde de la Médina, which seeks to preserve and restore the area. Displays include a map of the town showing how it looked in 1881. North of the *médina* the **Fort d'Espagne** (Spanish Fort, which was actually built by the Turks in the 1570s) offers an excellent view over Bizerte. The main beach runs for 5km alongside the route de la Corniche to Cap Bizerte.

Kasbah
- North of the Old Harbour
- Tue–Sun 9–12:30, 2:30–6 in winter (2:30–8 in summer)
- Cheap

Musée Oceanographique
- Avenue Habib Bourguiba
- Tues–Sun 9–12:30, 2:30–6 in winter (to 8 summer)
- Cheap

Zaouia de Sidi Mokhtar
- Place Lahedine Bouchoucha
- Exhibitions
- Free

Fort d'Espagne
- Boulevard Hassan en Nouri
- Cheap

Colourful small fishing boats moored at the Old Port of Bizerte

28A6
60km south of Tabarka, 9km north of Jendouba
08 630554
Daily 8–7 (8:30–5:30 in winter)
Nearest cafés and restaurants at Jendouba
To Jendouba from Tunis or Bizerte (around 4 hours) and then taxi or ***louage*** (shared taxi)
Cheap

Above: *the monumental ruins of the Memmian Baths*
Opposite: *a good view of Tabarka from the Genoese fort across the bay*

BULLA REGIA

This Roman site is as remarkable as Dougga but, because it is less well known, it is never overrun with visitors, making it much more atmospheric. Neolithic tombs at the site suggest Bulla Regia was inhabited long before the Romans and it was certainly the capital of one of the short-lived Numidian kingdoms. After it was annexed by Emperor Hadrian in the 2nd century it became one of the wealthiest Roman cities in North Africa.

The rich wheat and olive merchants of the town used to escape the summer heat by retreating to underground villas. Some of these were paved with beautiful mosaics and though some of the best have been moved to the Musée du Bardo in Tunis (► 22, Top Ten), others remain, undisturbed for centuries. These include the mosaic of Venus and a cupid riding on dolphins at thc Maison d'Amphitrite (House of Amphitrite); and a mosaic of fishermen at the Maison de la Pêche (House of Fishing), the oldest surviving villa. La Maison de la Chasse (House of the Hunt) has an elegant colonnaded courtyard and a sophisticated private baths complex.

Bulla Regia's two most impressive public buildings are a small and beautifully-preserved theatre with special seating reserved for its most important citizens, and the imposing Memmian Baths close to the site entrance. The market square and forum are flanked by the ruins of two temples, to Isis and Apollo whose priceless collection of statues are also now at the Musée du Bardo. There is a small museum at the entrance to the site.

DID YOU KNOW?

The main road between Tunis and Bulla Regia largely follows the Mejerda Valley, which became a bloody battlefield during World War II. Hundreds of lives were lost when British and American troops clashed with the Germans at Mejez el Bab, about 40km east of Béja.

DOUGGA (► 16, TOP TEN)

JEBEL ICHKEUL NATIONAL PARK (► 19, TOP TEN)

TABARKA ✪✪✪

Tabarka is Tunisia's flagship resort on the north coast. During the late 1980s and early 1990s the Tunisian government invested heavily in the town, building an international airport nearby. It is used regularly only in summer, bringing in mainly German and Italian holidaymakers. Nestled beneath the Kroumirie Mountains which are still covered with cork oaks, pine and eucalyptus, the town is not without charm, offering a long, unspoilt stretch of sandy beach to the east of the centre and to the west, a series of small rocky coves. The area is developing a reputation as a watersports centre with quality facilities for sailing, diving and windsurfing. Tunnels Reef (20 minutes by boat from Tabarka) is an extraordinary complex of tunnels, caves, caverns and gullies. Tabarka also has an 18-hole golf course.

The town began life as a Phoenician settlement and prospered in Roman times as a trading port. Modern-day Tabarka was largely designed by the French, who also built the causeway connecting the island of Tabarka to the mainland. The focal point of the town is avenue Habib Bourguiba where most of the shops and restaurants are to be found. The old port has been expanded into a luxury marina, Porto Corallo, and across the water is a 16th-century Genoese fort which is being prepared to house a small archaeological collection. The **Musée du Liège** (Cork Museum) 2km outside town on the Ain Draham road explains the industry and sells souvenirs.

- 28A6
- 175km from Tunis
- Hôtel de France (£), avenue Habib Bourguiba (► 92)
- Up to six buses daily to Tunis
- Tabarka Airport, 14km east of town
- Rue de Bizerte ☎ 08 671491 Mon–Thu 8:30–1 and 3–5:45. Fri, Sat 8:30–1:30. Closed Mon
- Few
- Université de l'Été is a festival of music, comedy and debates held in July. The annual Fête du Corail (Coral Festival), also held in July, is largely for tourists

Musée du Liège

- 2km out of town towards Aïn Draham
- Tue–Sun, 7–1, 3–6 (8–12, 2–5 winter)
- None
- Free

28A6
180km west of Tunis
Open access
At Ghardimaou
To Ghardimaou and then taxi
None
Free

THUBURNICA

Way out west, only 15km from the Algerian border, the Roman remains at Thuburnica are not exceptional and the journey is only for the really adventurous. The most intact remnant of the town is the beautiful Roman bridge crossing the bed of a river which carries the run-off from the surrounding hills in winter. This is still used to reach the ruins of the town itself. Visitors who know what they are looking for will see the remains of a couple of temples, a triumphal arch and parts of a two-storey mausoleum. At the top of the hill is a small Byzantine fort.

28B6
30km southeast of Bizerte
Daily 8–7 (8:30–5:30 in winter)
Picnic tables provided
Regular bus services between Tunis and Bizerte; get off at the turning about 2km from the site
None
Cheap

The site of Utica's public baths was huge, and much remains intact

UTICA

Equidistant between Tunis and Bizerte, Utica is now 10km from the sea though in Roman times it was an important port and the capital of the province of Africa. Much of the old Roman city lies buried under the deep mud of the Mejerda river which has been silting up for the past thousand years. The most intact part of the Roman remains is around La Maison de la Cascade (the House of the Waterfall) which obviously belonged to a very wealthy private citizen. The courtyard fountain, which gave its name to the house, still has remarkable mosaics.

The ruins of Utica's once-massive public baths complex still give an idea of how impressive they must once have been. Just in front of the entrance to the site there is a small museum containing pottery and other objects found at the baths.

Tunis to Jebel Ichkeul

An absorbing full-day itinerary which combines an unspoilt nature reserve and Roman ruins with one of the most striking and atmospheric towns in the country.

Head northwest out of Tunis on the A7 Tabarka road, through Jedeida to Mateur. Turn right towards Tinja and Menzel Bourguiba, following the signs to Lac Ichkeul.

The road becomes a track near the entrance to the park and at the gate visitors are asked to sign an official form (in French) promising to treat the countryside with respect.

Distance
180km

Time
8 hours including several stops

Start/end point
Tunis
28B6

Lunch
Le Sport Nautique (£££)
Boulevard Habib Bogatfa, Bizerte
02 431495

From the gate, it is another 3km to the car park for the Eco Museum and the starting point for various walks (► 19). Leave the park following signs for Bizerte. After 15km, take the turning to Menzel Bourguiba, the former French garrison town of Ferryville.

An atmospheric view of Lac d'Ichkeul, the heart of the Jebel Ichkeul National Park

The town was founded at the end of the 19th century to house European immigrants. Once nicknamed 'Little Paris', it has lost much of its charm but is worth a short stop on the way.

Return to the main Mateur–Bizerte road at the village of Tinja.

Fishermen can usually be seen battling to stop eel and mullet finding a way through the mesh of nets from Jebel Ichkeul to the open sea.

Head 20km north to Bizerte (► 40), the largest town on the north coast. Leave Bizerte on the A8 Tunis road. After 30km, there is a sign to the old Roman city of Utica (► 44). From Utica it is another 30km back to the centre of Tunis.

Cap Bon

Standing slightly apart from the rest of the country, the peninsula which ends at Cap Bon is the most productive in Tunisia. With a year-round mild climate, it is known as the Garden of Tunisia; there are citrus and olive groves, and vineyards – although this is a Muslim country there is a long tradition of wine-making, and a wine festival at Grombalia during the autumn grape harvest.

On old maps of Tunisia, the town of Nabeul is given as the focal point of the region. It remains the largest town and seat of local government, but in recent years it has been eclipsed by the relentless expansion of near-neighbour Hammamet – the most cosmopolitan resort in Tunisia and a firm favourite with package holidaymakers from all over Europe. In contrast, on Cap Bon's northern coast there are many small villages and long stretches of deserted beach without a hotel in sight.

> *'The earliest navigators rounded Cap Bon and the glorious prospect of the Gulf of Tunis was unfolded before their eyes, the emerald waters being separated from the golden sand by a delicate edging of white surf'*
>
> A. MACCALLUM SCOTT,
> *Tunis. A Medley of Races Under the French Flag* (1921)

Original columns and mosaic floors at the winter baths of Thuburbo Majus

Hammamet

28C5
60 km southeast of Tunis
To Tunis and Nabeul
One train a day between Tunis and Hammamet
Avenue Habib Bourguiba
02 280423

Tunisia's largest resort has been attracting package holidaymakers since the 1960s. Less than an hour's drive from Tunis–Carthage airport and only slightly more than that from Monastir–Skanès airport (the main arrival point for charter flights), Hammamet is geared up to year-round tourism and is equally popular with families and couples.

Easy-going and lively and with a good choice of restaurants, Hammamet's first hotels were built in the town centre close to the *médina* (► 49) but later developments stretch along the coast almost as far as Nabeul (► 52), making the most of some of the best beaches in the country.

The swimming pool of Sebastian's Villa, framed by whitewashed arches

What to See in Hammamet

CENTRE INTERNATIONAL CULTUREL ✪✪

Avenue des Nationes Unies
02 280065
8:30–6 (9–5 in winter)
None
Cheap
Festival of the Arts, Jul, Aug

Built by millionaire George Sebastian in the 1920s, Sebastian's Villa has been described as 'the most beautiful in the world' (ostensibly by Frank Lloyd Wright, and he should know). Guests have included Winston Churchill, Anthony Eden and the artist Paul Klee; Rommel used it as his headquarters during World War II. It is now used to stage an annual cultural festival each July and August and is also a venue for conferences and art exhibitions.

DAR HAMMAMET ✪

The *médina*
02 281206
8:30–7:30
None
Moderate

A small museum in the *médina* (► 49), filled with traditional costumes and a selection of bridal dowries from various parts of the country. The jewellery and embroidery are particularly impressive. There is a fine view of the modern town and the old *médina* from the rooftop terrace.

Hammamet's médina *is an atmospheric place to wander and shop*

KASBAH ✪✪

First built in the 15th century but heavily modified and restored since, the Kasbah is the best place to begin a tour of the *médina* (➤ below). The fort is Hammamet's most conspicuous landmark and is entered by way of a colossal ramp. There are steep steps up to the ramparts, from where there are fine views over the white domes and terraces of the *médina* and the surrounding coastline.

✉ The *médina*
🕒 8AM–9PM (8:30–6 in winter)
🍴 On the ramparts, the Café Turk (£)
♿ None
✋ Cheap

MÉDINA ✪✪✪

Much smaller than the *médinas* of Tunis (➤ 34), Sousse (➤ 62) and Sfax (➤ 73), but not without its charms, Hammamet's old town nestles around the Kasbah and Grande Mosquée (Great Mosque). It was built between 1463 and 1474 on the site of a 9th-century settlement. Although the streets closest to the *médina* walls are lined with souvenir shops there is a residential area which remains almost completely unspoilt. Wander through the narrow alleys – it's almost impossible to get lost. The studs on the doors are all individually designed and many incorporate the good luck symbols of fish and the hand of Fatima (the daughter of the Prophet Muhammed).

Immediately in front of the *médina* there is a market, and to the east is an ancient Muslim cemetery.

🍴 Café Sidi Bou Hdid, at the foot of the *kasbah* (➤ 95)
♿ None

PUPPUT ✪

Hammamet's only archaeological site consists of a couple of large Roman villas and a bath house paved with some fine mosaic floors. There are also 4th-century Christian tomb mosaics displayed on a perimeter wall. The ruins are all from the 2nd to the 4th centuries, when Pupput was a prosperous port.

✉ 6km south of the town centre
🕒 9–1, 3–7 (to 5:30 in winter)
🚌 No public transport
✋ Cheap

The Ghar el Kebir caves near El Haouaria

What to See in the Cap Bon region

EL HAOUARIA

- 28C6
- 14km northwest of Kerkouane
- Hotel Épervier (£–££)
  - rue Hedi Chaker
  - 02 297017
- Festival of falconry (Jun)

Just outside the village of El Haouaria are the spectacular Grottes Romaines (Roman Caves). On the seafront directly opposite the island of Zembra, there are 24 caves which were quarried for the soft orange limestone used by Carthaginian, Roman and Byzantine builders and sculptors. La Grotte des Chauves-Souris (Cave of the Bats), 4km from the town, is home to thousands of bats.

KÉLIBIA

- 28C6
- 68km northeast of Hammamet
- Restaurant Anis (£)
  - avenue Erriadh
  - 02 295777

Kélibia is a busy working town with a picturesque fishing port, still unspoilt by tourism and a good base for exploring the Cap Bon region. Overlooking the town is the giant Fort of Kélibia which was built in the 6th century. The ramparts offer excellent views over the harbour, coastline and surrounding countryside. Kélibia's main beach is 2km north of the town at Mansourah.

KERKOUANE

- 28C6
- 9km north of Kélibia
- 02 294033
- Tue–Sun 9–7 (9–4:30 in winter)
- Bus from Kélibia or taxi
- None
- Inexpensive

Dating from the 4th century BC, Kerkouane is a remarkable survival of a purely Punic town. It was destroyed in 236 BC and unearthed in 1952; it is now listed as a UNESCO World Heritage Site. Many of the houses had private bathrooms. The little museum has some beautiful jewellery, funerary statues and pottery.

KORBOUS

- 28C6
- 48km east of Tunis
- Several cafés (£) and Résidence des Thermes has a restaurant (££)
- Bus from Tunis
- None

A small spa town where people have come to 'take the waters' since Roman times. There are five springs including the hot and sulphurous Aïn el-Atrous (goat spring), said to be good for skin complaints and rheumatism. Women regularly slide down the nearby Zarziha Rock as a cure for infertility.

A Walk Around Nabeul

This leisurely walk offers an easy introduction to Nabeul (► 52–3).

Start at the Giant Orange Bowl on avenue Habib Thameur, a monument to the town's ceramic industry. Go past the regional hospital on the left before reaching the junction of avenue Farhat Hached and avenue Habib Bourguiba. Cross into avenue Farhat Hached.

This is a busy shopping street packed with shops and stalls selling everything from jeans and T-shirts to leather bags and suitcases.

Follow the road round to the left and after 150m turn left again into the covered souq. *Walk through to emerge facing one of the elaborate entrances to Nabeul's Grande Mosquée (Great Mosque).*

The lanes of the covered souq *lead to the Great Mosque*

Non-Muslims are barred from entry but walk round to the front for a glimpse of the courtyard. Note also the pretty tiled frontage of the house to the left of the mosque.

Cross the square, turn right into rue Souk el Ghezel and then right again into rue de France. With the Neapolis Center on the left, walk down the street and as you approach place des Martyrs – a formal public square with a fountain – turn left and through the gates of the bustling Marche Central.

The town's market is a riot of colour, sights and smells.

Return to place des Martyrs, turn left back into rue de France. After 250m head right into avenue Hedi Chaker, follow the road for 1km until a right-hand fork leads into rue Mohamed T'Latli and return to the Giant Orange Bowl.

Distance
3km

Time
2 hours allowing for shopping and drinks at the end

Start/end point
Giant Orange Bowl, Nabeul
28C5

Drinks
Café Errachida (£)
Avenue Habib Thameur
All day

NABEUL

28C5
65km southeast of Tunis
Hourly to Tunis; depart from bus station on avenue Habib Thameur
avenue Taieb Mehiri
02 286800

Neapolis
Opposite Hotel Monia Club, just off the *route Touristique*
8–1, 4–7 (9:30–4.30 in winter). Closed Mon
None
Cheap

Nabeul used to be known simply as Tunisia's pottery town but over the last decade or so it has rapidly developed as a resort in its own right and now has a clutch of large beach-front hotels. The main streets are crammed with pottery shops, souvenir stores and clothing boutiques, and every Friday the heart of the town is blocked off as Nabeul plays host to the so-called Camel Market. Drawing a good deal fewer camels than it does tourists, the event presents more of a chance for a shopping spree than anything else. For non-tourist goods the Marche Central (Central Market, ➤ 51) is much more genuine and well worth a visit.

In Roman times Nabeul's major industry was the manufacture of a pungent fish sauce called *garum* which was made by salting the blood and guts of tuna fish and then leaving it in an airtight container for three or four months. During excavations at Roman **Neapolis** on the outskirts of town during the 1960s several amphorae of the sauce were unearthed – but they appear to have passed their sell-by date. Neapolis is something of a

The Friday market in Nabeul attracts large crowds

disappointment if you have visited any of Tunisia's major archaeological sites – there is not much to see apart from a few pillars, some mosaic fragments and a series of pits thought to be the remains of a fish processing factory.

Nabeul's pottery industry also dates back to Roman times with many of today's designs and popular colours (blue and white, and yellow and green) the same as those used 2,000 years ago. Although pottery can be bought all over Tunisia Nabeul offers one of the biggest selections. Tourists who hate the idea of haggling can shop for pots and plates at two official tourist shops in the town (► 109) where all goods have fixed prices. (Even if you like the idea of haggling it is worth calling in at one of the shops just to get an idea of the true cost of items.) Do not be fooled by one or two other shops in the town displaying signs which suggest they too have set prices. It is just a ploy to entice visitors in – you will then find prices become surprisingly flexible.

Nabeul is a thriving centre for the manufacture of bricks and perfume, the suburb of Dar Chaabane specialises in stone carving and the village of Beni Khiar 2km to the east is known for its carpet weaving and wool products.

Exhibits at Nabeul's regional **Archaeological Museum**, directly opposite the railway station, include sculptures of the Carthaginian moon goddess Tanit unearthed in 1948 from a temple called Thinissut in the hills above Hammamet; some Carthaginian pieces excavated from Kerkouane (► 50); a 2,500-year-old statue of a naked man and a collection of Roman domestic pottery. In the courtyard there are a series of mosaics taken from the archaeological site at Neapolis illustrating episodes from Homer's *Iliad*.

The highly decorative Nabeul pottery is produced in many shapes and sizes

Archaeological Museum

✉ 44 avenue Habib Bourguiba

☎ 02 285509

🕐 8–1, 4–7 (9:30–4:30 in winter). Closed Mon

✋ Cheap

28B5
60km southwest of Tunis, 65km west of Hammamet
Daily 8–7 (8:30–5:30 in winter)
From Tunis to El Fahs and then taxi
Inexpensive

Below: *the extensive Roman ruins* , inset: *a relief of Pegasus*

THUBURBO MAJUS

First settled in the 5th century BC, most of the ruins at Thuburbo Majus are from later Roman times when the town was an important trading centre for the region's agricultural produce and probably had a population of around 8,000. Like many of Tunisia's archaeological sites, it is not unusual to have the place almost completely to yourself. With no guides available, even if you have a map, it can be quite difficult to make sense of the sprawling site.

The paved open space at the centre is the forum, which was where political and financial matters were discussed; the temple, built in AD 168, was dedicated to Jupiter, Juno and Minerva; the Winter Baths with their veined pink marble columns are up the hill. The Palaestra of the Petronii was a gymnasium (delineated by a line of columns) where young men took part in boxing or wrestling bouts. Many of the best finds from this site, including a statue of Jupiter and some fine mosaics, are now in the Musée du Bardo in Tunis (► 23, Top Ten).

28B5
30km west of Hammamet
Café at Temple des Eaux (£)
Frequent buses from Tunis, Nabeul and Hammamet

ZAGHOUAN

A sleepy, unspoilt agricultural town between Hammamet and Thuburbo Majus, with cobbled streets and tiled roofs. Dating from Roman times, water from Mount Zaghouan was used to supply Carthage by way of a 70km aqueduct, parts of which can still be seen along the Tunis–Zaghouan road. The Temple des Eaux (Temple of the Waters) built by the Emperor Hadrian in 130 is the town's greatest sight.

From Hammamet to Thuburbo Majus

An opportunity to combine spectacular Roman ruins with some unspoilt Tunisian countryside.

Head out of Hammamet on the main road towards Tunis. At the junction with the motorway follow the Zaghouan sign. On the outskirts of Zaghouan (➤ 54) follow signs for 'Centre Ville' turning left at the pharmacy and driving up the steep hill to the old town. Follow signs for Hôtel les Nymphes, turning right at Club de Chasse.

The Temple des Eaux (➤ 54) is surrounded by 12 empty niches which used to hold statues depicting the months of the year.

Turn left following signs to Tunis and El Fahs. After 12 km, immediately after the 'Welcome to El Fahs' sign, turn right and then left following the signs for Thuburbo Majus.

Allow at least an hour to look round the site (➤ 54).

Turn right out of the site, turning left after 1km on to the main Tunis road. Drive through the village of Bir M'Cherga and soon after take the right fork. After 25km, there is a right-hand turning towards Oudna.

As you pass by note the well-preserved remains of the Roman aqueduct, which carried water from Zaghouan to Carthage.

After 6km turn right towards Mornag. Follow signs to Grombalia, crossing a rickety metal bridge only big (and safe) enough for one vehicle at a time. Turn right after 3km and follow signs for Bouficha. Just after the village of Oued Ezzit turn left towards Hamman Jedidi and the road back to Hammamet.

Distance
200km

Time
7–8 hours including stops

Start/end point
Hammamet
28C5

Lunch
Picnic lunch at Thuburbo Majus or beside the Roman aqueduct at Oudna

Jebel Zaghouan stands high above the surrounding country

Food & Drink

Tunisian cuisine is typically North African and is influenced by Islamic traditions as well as by its Berber culture, using powerful spices and plenty of vegetables and fish. The French colonial heritage has produced some excellent wines.

Dried beans and peas of many varieties are a staple part of Tunisian cuisine

Although international food is served in most Tunisian tourist hotels many holidaymakers will want to try at least some local cuisine. The Arabs, Turks and French have all had an influence on the country's cooking. Fish is given pride of place on any menu and restaurant owners compete with each other to display the freshest catch. Bream, grouper, sea bass and red mullet are among the most widely available, while seafood speciality dishes are based on prawns, lobster and squid. Tuna is added to everything – even when you ask for a vegetarian pizza or green salad! Eggs are another staple ingredient which appear unexpectedly in many dishes.

A Typical Tunisian Meal

In all but the cheapest restaurants customers are nearly always welcomed with complimentary *hors d'oeuvres* which may be as simple as a bowl of black olives and some delicious crusty bread. In most places the bread will also be accompanied with a small saucer of fiery red *harissa* paste made from hot chillies (caution is advised).

A very popular starter is the famous *brik*, a unique Tunisian dish which consists of a triangular-shaped envelope of crispy pastry containing a lightly cooked egg and often topped with fresh herbs, prawns or – of course – tuna. It can only really be eaten with the fingers but beware of the yolk making a sudden and undignified escape. Safer starters include *ojja*, which are scrambled eggs mixed with tomatoes, pimentos, peppers and garlic. *Mechouia* consists of diced onions, red peppers and tomatoes mixed with olive oil, grilled and then served with

hard-boiled eggs and tuna. *Chorba* is a spicy soup of tomatoes, onions and *harissa* with tiny grains of pasta.

The obvious main course is *couscous*, a tasty vegetable, meat or fish stew served on a bed of steamed semolina grains, Tunisia's national dish. *Mesfuf* is a sweet *couscous* made with nuts and raisins. *Mechoui* (not to be confused with *mechouia*) is a plate of grilled meat, typically lamb chops with liver and *merguez* sausages generously laced with chilli.

Makroud, *a sweet and sticky pastry filled with dates, is a Kerouan speciality*

Dessert is often a choice of fresh fruit or very sweet pastries like *baklava* (pastry with nuts and honey) or *kab el ghazal* (a horn-shaped pastry filled with almonds).

What to Drink

Although Tunisia is a Muslim country alcohol is quite freely available in hotels and restaurants in Tunis and the main beach resorts. Bars outside hotels are male-dominated which may make women feel uncomfortable. Although a new German beer, *Berbere*, brewed in Hammamet, is slowly becoming available, most bars still only serve *Celtia*, a pleasant enough lager when served sufficiently cold. Some bars are also starting to serve local table wines by the bottle. The best red is the full-bodied Vieux Magon which is like a powerful shiraz, while the very dry Blanc de Blanc goes well with fish and seafood.

Tunisia's best-known spirits are *Thibarine*, a sweet, aromatic date liqueur and *boukha*, a fig brandy.

Couscous, traditional in Berber cuisine, is now Tunisia's national dish

Central Tunisia

Central Tunisia is a booming holiday region, combining two distinctive landscapes with a trio of colourful cities and a major Roman site. Sfax and Sousse are a delight with their ancient city walls, vibrant *souqs*, fascinating museums and thriving fishing ports. In the Islamic world their importance is overshadowed by Kairouan which is at the heart of the country in every sense. Tunisia's most holy city combines its spiritual role as a national centre for prayer and pilgrimage with the secular demands of its commercial carpet-making industry.

The surrounding richly fertile plain, known as the Sahel, stretches down the central east coast embracing the resorts of Mahdia and Monastir. Its vast numbers of olive trees have been the mainstay of the region's economy since Roman times. In contrast, the western Tell, once forested, is now a hauntingly desolate terrain only suitable for rough grazing. Its main attraction is the isolated Roman ruin of Sbeïtla.

'We quenched our thirst with tea in order to proceed in the dignified manner fitting for discovering such marvels'

PAUL KLEE
Describing his first trip to Kairouan, 1914

Tourists can try their hand at parascending from the water's edge

28C5
143km from Tunis
From Tunis
To Monastir
Buses to south and north
1 avenue Habib Bourguiba 03 225157 7:30AM–7.00PM (8:30–1, 3–5:30 in winter). Morning opening only Fri, Sat. Closed Sun
Plenty of choice (£–£££)

Sousse

Sousse used to be just an excursion destination for day trippers; now it is a busy holiday centre in its own right. Packed with atmosphere and hundreds of years of history, Tunisia's leading city beach resort offers good quality hotels, a wide choice of affordable restaurants and endless possibilities for shopping.

With Carthage (➤ 36) and Utica (➤ 44), Sousse was one of the Phoenicians' three great coastal cities, with the earliest archaeological finds dating from the 6th century BC. In the 7th century AD the city fell to Arab invaders who left it in ruins, but in 790 the foundations for a new city were laid, and many remnants of this time still survive today.

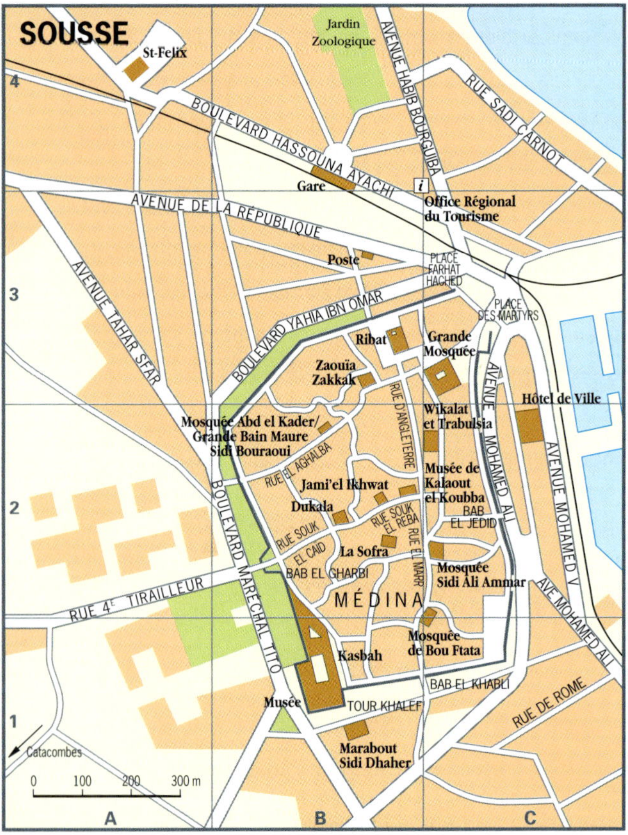

What to See in Sousse

CATACOMBS ✪

The catacombs could be developed into a major tourist attraction but for the moment their appeal is limited. There are purported to be more than 15,000 marble tombs from the 2nd to the 5th centuries spread throughout a 5.5km network of tunnels but currently only one very small section is open to the public.

60A1 (arrowed)
About 1km west of the *médina*, off rue Abdou Hamed el Ghazali
8–12, 3–7 (9–12, 2–6 in winter). Closed Mon
Cheap

GRANDE BAIN MAURE SIDI BOURAOUI ✪✪

The Sidi Bouraoui Baths is one of the best places to try a traditional *hammam* or *bain maure* (Turkish bath) with lengthy separate sessions for men and women. In a country where not everyone has a private bathroom but where personal hygiene is taken very seriously the *hammam* plays an important role in Tunisian society. For tourists it offers an interesting insight into local culture, is a chance to meet local people and, most importantly, is a healthy, relaxing and pleasurable way to spend two or three hours. The masseur (or for women, a masseuse) uses a coarse glove known as a *tfal* which leaves the skin pink and tingling.

60B2
Rue el Aghlaba (behind Mosquée Abd el Kader).
4AM–3PM for men; 3PM–midnight for women
Cheap

Above: *the beautiful city and historic port of Sousse*

GRANDE MOSQUÉE ✪✪✪

Respectful dress is required for a visit to the Great Mosque, which looks like a fortress with turrets and crenellations. Originally built in 851 by a freed slave called Mudam on the orders of the Aghlabite ruler Abdul Abbas, the internal courtyard has the pleasantly uncomplicated architecture common to many Islamic places of worship, the only decoration being a single line of Koranic inscription. A wide stairway leads to the walls; the minaret and prayer hall are not open to non-Muslims.

60C3
Rue el-Aghlaba
Daily 8–2. Closes early on Fri for noon prayers, and all day Sun
None
Cheap

60B1
Off boulevard Marechal Tito
03 233695
8–12, 4–7 (9–12, 2–6 in winter). Closed Mon and public holidays
None
Moderate

KASBAH SOUSSE MUSEUM ✪✪✪

Situated in the southwest corner of the *médina* (➤ below) the Kasbah Sousse Museum not only offers a superb panoramic view across the city, but has a fine and most interesting collection of mosaics rivalling those at the Musée du Bardo (➤ 23, Top 10). Most of the mosaics date from the 3rd and 4th centuries with the depiction of the Triumph of Bacchus among the most noted. The adjoining courtyard is a pleasant place to sit amongst the palm trees, flowers and bits of marble column and stone tablets.

60B2
Many cafés (£)
None

MÉDINA ✪✪✪

The *médina* is the old heart of Sousse and the area of the city with the greatest appeal. Its 9th-century walls are still largely intact apart from the area around the former sea gate at place des Martyrs, which was destroyed by the Allies during World War II – a testament to the continuing strategic importance of the city.

The *médina*'s biggest attractions are the Grande Mosquée (➤ 61), the *ribat* (➤ 63) and the Kasbah Museum (➤ above). Equally evocative and rewarding, however, is its overall ambience. Despite the increasing impact of tourism, the *médina* has retained a considerable amount of charm and character. The main shopping street runs from east to west from Bab Jedid to Bab el Gharbi. Halfway along, as the thoroughfare changes its name from rue Souq el Reba to rue Souq el Caïd, is a small warren of covered *souqs* selling everything from food and clothes to perfume and jewellery.

52B2
Rue Souq el Reba
9–1, 4–6:30 Mon–Thu, 9–2 Sat, Sun. Closed Fri
None
Cheap

Above: *haggling over souvenirs in the rue d'Angleterre in the Médina of Sousse*

MUSÉE DE KALAOUT EL KOUBBA ✪

The Museum of Kalaout el Koubba is in one of the most unusual buildings in the *médina* (➤ above) with a striking zigzag decoration on the dome. Dating from around the 11th century and believed to have been either an audience chamber for a neighbouring Fatimid palace or one of the hot rooms of a *hammam*, it has had many uses over the years, most recently as an art gallery and café. Today the museum's displays focus on the traditional life of the *médina* with ceramics, kitchen equipment, musical instruments and national costumes.

The main gate and circular tower of the Byzantine ribat *in Sousse*

RIBAT ✪✪✪

The *ribat* was built early in the 9th century as one of a chain of fortresses stretching along the Mediterranean coast to defend North Africa from European invaders. It was completed by the Aghlabids in 821, incorporating an earlier structure built in 790 which itself was sited on the ruins of a 6th-century Byzantine fortress. The large central courtyard which slopes downwards to a cistern is surrounded by a series of small cells which were used by the warrior-monks as tiny study-bedrooms.

A room above the main gate has four slits in the floor through which boiling olive oil was poured on unwelcome visitors. For many visitors, though, the most interesting part of the *ribat* is the view from the ramparts over the *médina* (► 62). There is often a queue to climb the 75 steps to the top of the circular tower for views of the town.

- 60B3
- Rue el Aghlaba
- Daily 8–7 (8–5:30 in winter)
- None
- Moderate

DID YOU KNOW?

If you are in Sousse on a Sunday there is a large open-air market which sprawls endlessly along the Sousse–Sfax road and draws a huge crowd. It is said to be possible to buy anything from a car to a camel – although most people make rather smaller purchases.

From Sousse to El Jem

Distance
160km

Time
Seven hours including stops

Start/end point
Sousse
60C5

Lunch
Scandinavia Corner Cafeteria (£) for sandwiches and snacks
Opposite the entrance to the amphitheatre

This scenic drive includes the tourist town of Monastir (➤ 68) and is ideal for holidaymakers looking for a day trip from Sousse (or Port El Kantaoui, ➤ 70). Starting soon after breakfast is recommended.

Head southwest out of Sousse past the louages station following signs to Sfax and Kairouan. Drive through the suburbs of Zaouiet Sousse and Messadine. Soon after leaving M'Saken join the A1 and head south on a long, straight road flanked by row upon row of olive trees.

It takes just over an hour to get to El Jem (➤ 17, Top Ten) driving at a leisurely pace. It is impossible to miss the amphitheatre which dominates the small town and can be seen clearly from the approach road. Finding somewhere to park may be more difficult. Allow a good 90 minutes for the amphitheatre and a quick walk around town.

At the top of the main street, at the furthest point from the amphitheatre, turn left, taking the Mahdia road out of El Jem. Drive for 10km passing through the village of Telelsa and then turn left at the signpost for Moknine. Reaching a crossroads after about 12km head straight on into the village of El Fhoul, reaching Moknine 16km later. Follow the signs to Monastir 30km further north.

The extravagant mausoleum of Habib Bourguiba, seen from the tower of the ribat in Monastir

The *ribat* and Bourguiba Mausoleum are among Monastir's main tourist attractions (➤ 68–9). The town is also good for souvenir shopping.

Head out of town following signposts for Tunis. Take the A1 north for the easy 20km drive back to Sousse.

What to See in Central Tunisia

EL JEM (➤ 17, TOP TEN)

ILES KERKENNAH (➤ 18, TOP TEN)

KAIROUAN (➤ 20–1, TOP TEN)

LE KEF ✪✪✪

Le Kef – which means 'rock' in Arabic – refers to the town's dramatic setting on a rocky outcrop just below the summit of Jebel Dyr. Considered to be the capital of the Tell region which covers much of Central Tunisia, Le Kef is Tunisia's most significant inland centre after Kairouan. This was a fortress town from 450 BC, and tools have been found in surrounding caves and woodland dating back 50,000 years. In Roman times Le Kef became an important trading post and over the last thousand years it has been involved in numerous border wars and disputes. During World War II it served as headquarters for the Free French.

Aïn el Kef is a spring which may well have been the reason for a town being built here; it has been venerated for centuries and a small shrine still attracts votive offerings. Le Kef has two ***kasbahs*** which are linked by a drawbridge and enclosed by a wall. The older, larger fort was first built in Byzantine times and later remodelled by the Turks; the other was built in the early 19th century. Jemaa el Kebir (Old Mosque) was one of the oldest mosques in Tunisia but is now closed. Next to it the Mosquée de Sidi Bou Makhlouf was built at the beginning of the 17th century and is named after the town's patron. The **Musée Regional des Arts et Traditions Populaires** (Regional Museum of Popular Arts and Traditions) focuses on the culture of the Berber people with displays of clothes, jewellery and household objects.

Below: *the fortifications at Le Kef*

28A5
170km southwest of Tunis
To Tunis from the Gare Routiere SNT
The Artisanat Dar El Medina (The Association for the Protection of the Medina) acts as an informal tourist office: rue Hedi Chaker
Hotel-Restaurant Venus (££) Junction of rue Farhat Hached and avenue Habib Bourguiba 08 200355

Kasbahs

Daily 7–5. Closed Mon
Free

Musée Regional des Arts et Traditions Populaires

Place Ben Aissa
08 221503
9–1, 4–7 (9:30–4:30 in winter)
Cheap

MAHDIA ✪✪

28C5
205km from Tunis, 62km from Sousse
Cafés in place du Caire (£)
Three services a day from Tunis from the station on avenue Farhat Hached
Almost hourly buses to Sousse and Sfax
Rue el Moez (just inside the *médina* by the Skifa el-Kahla) 03 681098
Few

Regional Museum of Mahdia
Place de l'Indépendance
9–12, 2–6 (9:30–4:30 in winter). Closed Mon
None
Moderate

Borj el Kebir
Rue du Borj
9–12, 2–6 (9:30–4:30 in winter). Closed Mon
None
Cheap

The entrance to the newly built mosque in Mahdia

Set on a peninsula and still clinging to its old way of life with its weaving industry and thriving fishing port, Mahdia's small *médina* is the most obvious sign of the town's changing fortunes. Nearly every shop and stall is now geared towards tourists since the creation of a burgeoning *zone touristique* 6km west of the town centre, where the best beaches are to be found.

Mahdia's history dates from the 10th century when it was the capital of the Fatimid dynasty. All that remains of the town's fortifications is the Skifa el-Kahla (the Dark Gate), which stands at the entrance to the *médina*. Next to it is the new **Regional Museum of Mahdia**, with archaeological exhibits from Punic, Roman and Fatimid times and a collection of traditional costumes.

Take a walk along the main thoroughfare, the rue Obidallah el Mehdi. At the end of the street there is the peaceful place du Caire where cafés, some with seats shaded by trees and vines, serve refreshments throughout the day. Just beyond the square is the Grande Mosquée (Great Mosque), but do not be fooled by its aged appearance – it was only built in the 1960s and is a replica of the thousand-year-old original. The large fortress which stands on the highest point of the peninsula is the **Borj el Kebir**, a 16th-century Turkish fort which offers excellent views over the town, port and surrounding Muslim cemetery. The port may look familiar: it was used as the setting for the German invasion of Benghazi in the Oscar-winning film *The English Patient*.

A Walk Around Mahdia

Distance
4km

Time
Two hours including stops

Start point
Fishing port
28C5

End point
Rue des Fatmides
28C5

Lunch or coffee
Café Sidi Salem (£)
rue du Borj

This walk can be done at any time of the day but is particularly recommended in the early morning.

Start at the fishing harbour, which is still the focal point of Mahdia despite the onslaught of tourism.

Allow some time to wander around the harbour to watch fishermen unload the catch or repair their nets; call in at the slippery-floored fish maket where traders auction fish straight from the sea.

Turn right out of the harbour entrance on to the seafront path which leads to the Grande Mosquée (Great Mosque) and Borj el Kebir (► 66). With the fort on your left, branch off to walk through the cemetery with its simple white gravestones. Follow the path round to the tiny red lighthouse passing the gardens and rocks off to the right which form Cap d'Afrique. Turning the corner of the windswept headland, notice the whitewashed roofs of the zone touristique *in the distance. Walk back towards Mahdia town along a narrow street of traditional seafront houses.*

The old port of Mahdia, protected by the lighthouse on Cap d'Afrique

You will pass the Artisanat Dar El Médina on the left, which offers information about the *médina* and is located in an attractive house on avenue 7 Novembre.

Turn left up the alleyway running alongside the Hotel Al-Jazira. Follow it around to emerge next to the tourist information centre and the main entrance to the médina. *Stroll down rue Obidallah el Mehdi to the shaded place du Caire and then turn right by the side of Mosquée Mustapha Hamza which leads to a cluster of shops and cafés on rue des Fatmides.*

Monastir

Until the 1960s Monastir was a fairly typical Tunisian town, but it has been transformed into a showpiece tourist resort of pristine streets, elegant turn of the century lampposts and an abundance of greenery. It has an attractive 400-berth marina and an old fishing port. Most of Monastir's tourist hotels are located 6km west of the town centre in the suburb of Skanès near the international airport.

28C5
160km south of Tunis
From Sousse
Frequent departures to Sousse
Rue de l'Indépendance
8:30–1, 3–5:45 Mon–Thu; 8:30–1.30 Fri, Sat. Closed Sun
Also Monastir Airport 03 461205 24 hrs

What to See in Monastir

BOURGUIBA MOSQUÉE

In the early years of his presidency, the Republic of Tunisia's first leader Habib Bourguiba built himself an elaborate mausoleum here in the centre of the town of his birth. Instantly recognisable by its twin minarets and golden dome, it has an impressive tree-lined drive leading to the gates; at its foot is a kiosk commemorating those who died fighting for Tunisia's independence. A golden statue of the schoolboy Bourguiba stands in the nearby place du Gouvernorat.

Top end of Sidi el Mazeri Cemetery
Closed to visitors

Above: *the massive* ribat *of Harthema stands above the harbour at Monastir*

MÉDINA

A great chunk of Monastir's *médina* was demolished in the 1960s in the course of a misguided modernisation plan, and with it the Old Town district lost much of its heart. Dedicated to protecting the *médina* from any further development (a somewhat lost cause) is the **Association de Sauvegarde de Médina** (City Safe-Keeping Association). Its centre, built around a whitewashed courtyard shaded by an orange tree, provides a welcome oasis from the surrounding bustle.

Association de Sauvegarde de Médina
Rue du 2 Mars
9–1. 3–7 (9–12, 2–6 in winter). Closed Mon
Special exhibitions occasionally mounted

MUSÉE DES ARTS ET TRADITIONS ✪✪

Refurbished in 1996, the stone-floored, somewhat spartan Museum of Arts and Traditions contains a collection of impressive outfits worn by couples on their wedding day – and for many days following the ceremony. In the 18th and 19th centuries it was traditional for the bride's dress to be made by her mother and sisters, which sometimes took several years because of the huge amount of intricate embroidery involved. The men's costumes are much simpler. The costumes are attractively presented in glass-fronted cabinets, with a display of costume jewellery.

Rue de l'Indépendance
9–1, 3–7. Closed Mon
Cheap

RIBAT ✪✪✪

Founded in 796, the *ribat* has been reworked and restored so many times that there is little left of the original structure. One surviving section from earliest times is the prayer hall which is now used as a **Museum of Islamic Arts**. Exhibits include fragments of 12th-century weaving, Egyptian fabrics, samples of Islamic writings and a gold jewellery collection from Persia. The Nador tower offers spectacular views over the town centre and corniche.

The *ribat* has provided the backdrop for scenes in several major films including *Jesus of Nazareth* and *The Life of Brian*. Connected to the southern gate is the Grande Mosquée (Great Mosque), built at the same time as the *ribat* and *médina* walls. It is closed to non-Muslims.

Behind the route de la Corniche
03 461272
8–7 (9:30–7 in winter)
Moderate (includes entry to Museum of Islamic Arts)

The Nador tower gives spectacular views over Monastir

28C5
134km south of Tunis
Buses to Sousse operate along the main road just outside the entrance to Port El Kantaoui
The marina 8:30–1, 3–5:45 Mon–Thu. 8:30–1:30 Fri, Sat. Closed Sun
Les Emirs (£££), The marina 03 240865

Above: *the recently built resort town of El Kantaoui is focused on the marina*

PORT EL KANTAOUI ✪✪

Port El Kantaoui arouses quite strong feelings between those who love the resort and those who are rather less keen. Purpose-built around a picturesque marina which now draws luxury yachts from all over the world, it opened in 1979 and has been Tunisia's most outstandingly successful tourist centre.

With the look and feel of an elite residential district, it is the sort of development where you would expect to find the homes of top politicians, diplomats or the fabulously wealthy. The only difference is that the residents of this smart enclave are mainly package holidaymakers, often first-time visitors looking for a gentle introduction to Tunisia. Equally popular with families and older couples who like its reassuringly familiar ambience and strong sense of safety, detractors criticise Port El Kantaoui for its artificiality. It's also not unusual to find holidaymakers outnumbering Tunisians ten to one.

Millions of dinars have been poured into landscaping, with palm trees, shrubs and grass borders lining every road and not a tatty bit of paintwork in sight. The resort's hotels are equally sparkling; giant whitewashed palaces with their own terraced gardens awash with bougainvillaea.

DID YOU KNOW?

If you want to get from Port El Kantaoui to Sousse and don't want to take a taxi, you can ride in an open-sided 'Noddy Train' which is very popular with children. It operates hourly daytime services between the two resorts, leaving from the main entrance to the Kantaoui marina in front of the imitation fort.

The early built hotels have the advantage of being closest to the marina and are also generally thought to offer the best quality. Some of the newest accommodation can involve a good ten-minute walk to the shops and restaurants surrounding the harbour. Port El Kantaoui is practically self-sufficient and apart from the obligatory souvenir shops it has banks, a supermarket, hairdressers and a newsagent.

Sailing trips in glass-bottomed cruisers, fishing boats or in an imitation pirate's galleon are available from the marina. There is also a diving club and nearby riding stables have horses and camels for hire. Port El Kantaoui's pride and joy is its beautifully manicured 36-hole championship golf course (► 113). There are no membership requirements and while golfers with their own equipment are welcome, those who prefer to travel light can hire everything from clubs to caddies at very reasonable rates. Most hotels will arrange bookings and pre-set tee-times with the club.

The Temple of Jupiter catches the evening sun at Sufetula near Sbeïtla

SBEÏTLA ✪✪

If it were not for its impressive Roman ruins, Sbeïtla would attract very few visitors. Far from any tourist resort, Sbeïtla is the most southerly of Tunisia's major Roman sites. Established at the beginning of the first century on what had been an early Numidian settlement, it was known as Sufetula and reached the height of its prosperity towards the end of the 2nd century. By then it had a population of more than 10,000 people, double the number of people who live in Sbeïtla today.

There is a massive triumphal arch just before the entrance to the archaeological site; other interesting ruins include the much-photographed forum built in 139, the well-preserved baths with their ingenious under-floor heating system and a more modern structure, the 6th-century Basilica of St Vitalis with a beautiful baptismal font covered in mosaics.

28B5
117km west of Kairouan
7–7 (8:30–5:30 in winter)
Three buses a day to Kairouan from a car park on the southern edge of town, off rue Habib Thameur
None
Moderate

- 28C4
- 270km southeast of Tunis
- Five services a day (four in winter) to El Jem, Sousse and Tunis from the station at the eastern end of avenue Habib Bourguiba.
- To Tunis and Sousse
- Regular daytime services to Iles Kerkennah
- Four Tuninter flights a week to Tunis
- Avenue Mohamed H Khefacha (near the ferry port for Kerkennah) 04 211040 7:30–1, 3–5:45 (8:30–1, 3–5:45 in winter)
- Socopa Craft Shop rue Hammadi Taj 04 296826 9–12, 4–7 (9–12, 3–6 in winter)

Above: *the massive defensive walls of the old town of Sfax*

Sfax

Tunisia's second city is rarely visited by holidaymakers except perhaps those with a couple of hours to spare while awaiting ferries to Iles Kerkennah (➤ 18). Although it is mainly an industrial city with factories sprawling along the coastline, the city centre is attractively compact and very underrated. To the south of Sfax is an evocative Commonwealth War Cemetery, 2km down the Gabès Road.

Founded in 849 near the site of a small Roman town, Taparura, Sfax quickly became prosperous by trading in the products of the Sahel's olive trees. Remaining largely independent until the beginning of the 17th century it strongly resisted the imposition of the French Protectorate in 1881 which led to French marines storming the city defacing its mosques and killing several hundred people. Hedi Chaker and Farhat Hached, two of the Tunisia's trade union leaders involved in securing the country's independence and whose names are seen on street signs across the country, both hailed from Sfax.

What to See in Sfax

- Junction of avenues Habib Bourguiba and Hedi Chaker
- 04 229744
- Tue–Sat, 9:30–4:30
- Cheap

ARCHAEOLOGICAL MUSEUM

The archaeological collection is housed on the ground floor of the Town Hall, an unmistakable colonial building with a dome and clock tower. Although it only comprises six exhibition rooms there are several items of interest including an unusual 3rd-century Roman mosaic of children wrestling, Christian funerary mosaics and Roman and Muslim tombs. There are also displays of Roman wall paintings, glass and prehistoric tools from Gafsa (➤ 83).

MÉDINA ✪✪✪

The old town in Sfax has one of the best-preserved and most atmospheric *médinas* in the country. Surrounded by massive stone walls originally built by the Aghlabites in the 9th century, it is a hive of activity with dozens of first-floor workshops for tailors, engravers and furniture-makers. At the heart of a labyrinth of narrow streets and *impasses* is the Grande Mosquée (Great Mosque), which was started in 849 and extensively rebuilt in the 10th century. Closed to non-Muslims, the best view of its celebrated, several-tiered minaret is from place Souk el Djemaa.

Sfax's covered *souqs* run between the Grande Mosquée and rue des Forgerons. Immediately beyond Bab Jebli, the oldest surviving gateway to the *médina*, is a large food market. Go early in the day as the night's fishing catch is unloaded from cold storage vans. An even bigger daily fish market operates opposite the docks on avenue Ali Bach Hamba.

Main entrance on avenue Ali Belhouane
Many cafés (£)
Free

MUSÉE REGIONAL DES ARTS ET TRADITIONS ✪✪

The Regional Museum of Arts and Traditions (also known as the Dar Jallouli museum), is at the heart of the *médina* in a handsome 17th century townhouse, the former home of one of Tunisia's most influential families, and gives an idea of what life would have been like for an upper class family in Sfax in the 19th century. The house itself is just as interesting as the exhibits, with its white paved floors, tiled walls and carved wood ceilings. As well as displays of furniture, traditional costumes and jewellery, there are special sections on calligraphy and painting on glass.

Rue de le Driba
04 211186
9–4:30. Closed Mon
Cheap

Below: *narrow alleyways honeycomb the* médina *in Sfax*

In the Know

If you want to get the real flavour and feel of the country, here are some ideas.

10 Ways to be a Local

Learn a few words of Arabic – it works wonders and is well worth the effort for the obvious pleasure it brings.

Avoid talking politics or making any criticism of the President, whose photograph appears everywhere.

Eat in a *gorgote* or *rôtisserie* and enjoy the value for money.

Buy a *burnous* – a long woollen coat with a hood which is very useful in the winter when it can turn extremely cold in the north.

Smoke a *chicha* (hookah pipe) while playing a game of cards in a smoky, starkly lit café or bar.

Never switch on your car headlights until it is pitch black assuming that because you know you are on the road everyone else must be able to see you.

Get up at sunrise and consider you are having a late night if you are still out on the town at 10PM.

Don't worry about being under-dressed – even deluxe hotels rarely insist on a jacket and tie.

Be prepared for the incessant ringing of mobile phones; conversations will be conducted at a decibel level which would seem to make their use superfluous.

Don't drive past a hitch-hiker if you have room to pick them up. Car ownership is rare and poor public transport in rural areas means hitch-hiking is common. It adds an extra dimension to a journey, and the gesture will be much appreciated.

10 Good Places to Have Lunch

Restaurant Bon Kif (££–£££) avenue Marbella (off avenue Habib Thameur), Nabeul ☎ 02 222783. Stylish Tunisian restaurant where tourists and locals gather for long, lazy lunches.

Fishing from a small boat is a way of life for many Tunisians

Boys enjoy a game of football in Belvedere Park, Tunis

Dar El Jeld (£££) rue Dar El Jeld, Tunis ☎ 01 260916. Superb Tunisian food in the setting of a sumptuous mansion.
La Daurade (££–£££) The Marina, Port El Kantaoui ☎ 03 244893. Very popular fish restaurant with shaded outside seating.
Le Lido (££) avenue Mohammed V, Sousse ☎ 03 225329. Sit outside opposite the harbour and enjoy fresh fish.
Les Margaritas (££) rue de Hollande, Tunis ☎ 01 240631. There is a theatrical feel about this perennially popular lunchtime venue.
RestoVert (£) avenue de la République, Hammamet. Soups, salads and sandwiches in a friendly café lined with movie posters.
Café Sidi Salem (£) rue du Borj, Mahdia. Sit outside and admire the expansive sea view.
La Sirine (£–££) avenue Assad ibn el Fourat, Hammamet. Everything from *crêpes* to *couscous* at this beach restaurant.
La Sirène (££) Remla beachfront, Iles Kerkennah ☎ 04 281118. Excellent fresh fish in a venue overlooking the sea.
Le Sport Nautique (£££) boulevard Habib Bougatfa, Bizerte ☎ 02 431495. Ideal for a leisurely lunch overlooking the entrance to the harbour.

10 Top Activities

Bathing Most Tunisians visit a *hammam* (Turkish bath) at least once a week.
Cinema-going A very popular pastime, even though most films are dubbed and long films heavily cut.
Cycling No better place than on the flat, uncrowded roads of Iles Kerkennah.
Diving Quality tuition and excellent dive sites in the waters around Tabarka.
Fishing A way of life for many Tunisians; no permit is required to fish from any of the harbours.
Football Tunisians are fanatical about football at all levels with Sunday the big day for local matches.
Four-wheel driving Ideal transport for exploring the desert region.
Golf Very high standards and eight courses to choose from.
Hunting Wild boar is hunted in winter in the forests around Tabarka.
Watersports Try waterskiing, paragliding and windsurfing in all the main beach resorts.

10 Places to Picnic

- Jebel Ichkeul National Park (➤ 19)
- Thuburbo Majus (➤ 54)
- Any of the deserted beaches on Iles Kerkennah (➤ 18)
- Parc du Belvédère, Tunis (➤ 35)
- The empty roadside near the desert villages of Chebika, Midès and Tamerza (➤ 82, 85, 86)
- Dougga (➤ 16)
- Bulla Regia (➤ 42)
- Carthage (➤ 26, 36)
- Sbeïtla (➤ 71)
- Thuburnica (➤ 44)

A poster advertising an Egyptian film; cinema-going is very popular

Jerba & the South

Apart from Jerba which offers some of the most unspoilt beaches in the Mediterranean and a charming pocket-sized capital, Houmt Souq, the desert region remains a well-kept secret. Covering much of the southern half of the country, it is beginning to attract more attention since the worldwide success of the Oscar-winning movie *The English Patient*, much of which was filmed around the oasis town of Tozeur. European holidaymakers usually prefer to visit the desert region in early spring or late autumn as the summer months can be oppressively hot.

Desert safaris from the east coast beach resorts rarely stay more than two or three nights in the region, with Tozeur the traditional focal point. Popular spots en route include Matmata with its unusual cave dwellings made famous in another big movie, *Star Wars*, and the Gorges de Selja, famous for the rail journey on Le Lezard Rouge (Red Lizard) train.

'I slipped into the orchards and experienced the cheerfulness of the fountains amidst the blossoming trees.'

SIMONE DE BEAUVOIR (1908–86) on seeing the oasis at Gabès.

The dramatic gorge of Midès in the far southwest

28C3
506km south of Tunis
Two services a day to Sousse, Sfax and Tunis
Up to seven Tuninter flights a day from Jerba to Tunis from Mellita airport
place des Martyrs, Houmt Souq 05 658116

Above: *a shady square in Houmt Souq, the main town on the island of Jerba*

Jerba

Thought to be the 'land of the Lotus Eaters', where Ulysses came ashore during his Odyssey, Jerba is the holiday destination of many Tunisians. It is the only beach resort in the country which can claim to be attractive year-round, though it can be quite chilly during the day from November to January with the temperature dropping further at night.

While its population is one of the most cosmopolitan in the country, Jerba society is deeply conservative and – confronted with the demands of foreign tourists – there remains a strong determination to preserve the island's distinct identity. Measuring just 29km wide by 27km long, Jerba is said to have 354 mosques – one for every day of the Islamic year.

What to See in Jerba

22km south of Houmt Souq
To Jorf every 30 minutes, 6am–midnight; every 2 hours, midnight–6AM
Cheap for cars; free for foot passengers

AJIM ✪✪

Visitors arriving by ferry dock at Ajim. Still an important centre for sponges, which are collected from the seabed by divers, it is also a busy fishing port. In the summer months there can be long queues for the car ferry to Jorf – a two-hour wait is not unusual. Swimming around Ajim is not recommended, as there are often swarms of jellyfish in this area.

7km long from southeast corner of Ile de Jerba to the mainland
Free

EL KANTARA CAUSEWAY ✪

Driving across the El Kantara Causeway is the alternative to taking the ferry to and from the mainland, but it adds around 100km to a journey. The first causeway was built in Carthaginian times and survived until 1551, when it was badly damaged by the Turkish pirate Dragut. Repairs were not made until 1953.

ERRIADH (HARA SEGHIRA) ✪

The only reason for coming here is to see the **El Ghriba Synagogue**, one of the most holy Jewish shrines in North Africa. There has been a strong Jewish presence in Tunisia, and particularly in Jerba, going back many centuries. Jerba's Jews today number around a thousand, many having migrated to Israel, and the synagogue now provides a meeting place for the ageing community. Suitably dressed visitors are welcome to enter the atmospheric synagogue with its bright blue pillars, dark wood panelling, painted tiles and stained glass.

8km from Houmt Souq

Buses from Houmt Souq to Guellala (► below) stop in Erriadh

El Ghriba Synagogue

1km from town centre

Daily. Closed Sat

None

Free

Left: *a potter at work in Guellala*

GUELLALA ✪✪

Guellala rivals Nabeul (► 52) as a pottery-producing centre. The clay for the pottery – all of which is handmade – is quarried from hills above the village and out towards nearby Sedouikech. The main street is lined with shops all piled high with pots and plates; there are several workshops and dozens of kilns. Haggle effectively and most pieces are very cheap, though quality varies enormously. Expect to pay more for anything with fish on it and look out for specialities such as camel-shaped water jugs. Guellala is a popular morning stop on coach tours of the island, so the best bargains can usually be negotiated in mid-afternoon when there are fewer people around.

The Mosquée de Guellala (1km out of town on the road to Erriadh) dates from the 15th century. On the same road, nearer El Kantara (► 78) is the crumbling ruin of the Mosquée de Sidi Yati which was built in the tenth century.

18km from Houmt Souq, 6km from El Kantara

Four buses a day from Houmt Souq

None

28C4
22km northeast of Ajim
Good choice (£–££)
Bus station on avenue Bourguiba
Boulevard de l'Environment 05 650016 and avenue Bourguiba 05 650915

Borj el Kebir
At the seafront end of rue Taieb Mehiri, 700m from the fishing port
8–12, 3–7 (9:30–4:30 in winter). Closed Fri
Cheap

Musée des Arts et Traditions Populaires
Avenue Abdelhamid el-Kadhi
05 650540
8–12, 3–7 (9.30–4.30 in winter). Closed Fri
Moderate

Above: *carpet market*
Opposite, top: *silver brooch from the museum*
Right: *ancient olive tree near Midoun*

HOUMT SOUQ

Houmt Souq, the capital of Jerba, is situated on the island's north coast 6km from the airport at Mellita. It is a charming place to spend few days and makes a good base for excursions to other parts of the island and further afield. Houmt Souq means 'marketplace', and this remains the town's primary purpose despite its now blossoming tourism industry, which has brought the inevitable crop of souvenir shops and European-style restaurants.

The heart of the town is the snug little complex of whitewashed squares and streets surrounding the *souq*, where goods including jewellery, coral and leatherware are sold. There is also a daily fish auction. Mondays and Thursdays are the busiest days when traders come in from all over the island to sell straw baskets and mats.

On the seafront, close to Houmt Souq's busy fishing harbour, is the **Borj el Kebir** (also known as Borj Ghazi Mustapha). There has probably been a fort here since Roman times, but the earliest remains are of a fortress built at the end of the 13th century by the Sicilian Roger de Loria. Most of the existing structure dates from the late 15th and early 16th centuries. In 1560 – when controlled by the Spanish – it was the scene of a famous two-month siege and massacre led by the Turkish pirate Dragut, who stormed the castle and killed all its occupants. The skulls of the defeated Spanish soldiers were dumped in an 11m-high pile close to the port; today a small white monument marks the spot.

Among several interesting mosques (all closed to non-Muslims) is the multi-domed Mosque of the Strangers, the Jami'et-Turuk (the Mosque of the Turks) which has a beautiful minaret and the Zaouia de Sidi Brahim which contains the tomb of a 17th-century saint.

The **Musée des Arts et Traditions Populaires** (Museum of Arts and Popular Traditions) is housed in a former mosque – the Zaouia de Sidi Zitouna. Dedicated to Jerban culture, it has a large collection of costumes and jewellery; a reconstruction of a pottery workshop with some huge jars which were used to store everything from grain to clothing; and another room is filled with antique wooden chests.

MIDOUN ✪✪

Jerba's second biggest town really springs into life on Friday – market day – when streets all around the centre are filled with makeshift stalls, attracting a large crowd of local people and tourists. Try to arrive as early as possible, because it is all but over by lunchtime. Another crowd-puller takes place on Tuesday afternoons, when a mock Berber wedding procession is held for the benefit of visitors.

- 28C3
- 16km east of Houmt Souq
- Several (£–££)
- Frequent from Houmt Souq and the tourist resorts

SIDI MAHREZ ✪✪

Starting at Flamingo Point about 8km east of Houmt Souq and extending as far as Ras Taguermes (marked by a lighthouse), this 10km stretch of coastline is said to be the best beach in Jerba. The *zone touristique* occupies some of this with its cluster of large hotels, but there are quieter areas. Another unspoilt stretch can be found south of Aghir while the wild and rocky west coast is almost totally uninhabited.

- 28C4
- 8–18km east of Houmt Souq
- Bar snacks at the beach hotels
- Bus from Houmt Souq

What to See in the South

28A4
60km northwest of Tozeur
No public transport; join an organised excursion or hire a car

Above: *steep limestone cliffs overlook the palmery at Chebika*

CHEBIKA

Chebika is the southernmost of three mountain villages close to the Algerian border which can be visited together on a day trip from Tozeur (► 87). The others are Midès (► 85) and Tamerza (► 86).

Abandoned after serious flooding in 1969, the old village of Chebika is now in ruins, but the villagers are making the most of tourism and still cultivate their gardens. There are guides available to lead you up the mountainside to see the waterfall which feeds the oasis; there is a good view of the salt lake of Chott el Gharsa.

28A3
Kebili is 120km west of Gabès
Small cafés in most oasis towns
Four a day from Gabès

CHOTT EL JERID

Chott el Jerid is the most southwesterly of a series of salt lakes lying inland of Gabès (► 83). This vast salt lake of shifting colours and mirages covers nearly 5,000sq km. Lifeless in summer, the water evaporates leaving a crust of salt crystals which glisten in the sun, brilliant white interspersed with patches of green, orange and pink, caused by the different chemical constituents of the salts. In winter water collects on either side of the raised causeway built across the Chott from Degache to Kebili (► Drive, 90) and life returns to this inland sea. The lake is fringed with small oasis towns, whose economy depends entirely on the cultivation of dates.

Journeys across the Chott used to be hazardous and all the tourist literature tells of a huge caravan wandering off the main route and disappearing through the thin surface. It's still advised not to go off the beaten track.

Opposite: *pomegranates ripen in a lush oasis near Gafsa*

DOUZ ✪✪✪

Douz is right on the edge of the desert as most northerners think of it – the dunes are not quite so impressive here as they are a bit deeper into the Eastern Desert but they are enough for most visitors. Just outside the town near the village of Gleissia is the so-called Great Dune where most tours stop. The town centre is transformed early on a Thursday morning into a frenetic weekly produce market which draws shoppers and traders from a wide area, selling everything from sheep, goats and camels, to dates, spices and beans, as well as clothing and leather goods.

The recently reopened **Douz Museum** explores the history and culture of the southern Jerid with costumes and jewellery, camel harnesses and a Bedouin tent.

28B3
148 km southwest of Gabès
Choice of cafés (£)
To Tunis, Douz and Kebili
Place des Martyrs 05 470351 8:30–1, 3–5:45 Mon–Thu. 8–1:30 Fri, Sat. Closed Sun. Also route de Zaafrane 05 470351 8:30–1, 3–5:45 Mon–Thu. 8–1:30 Fri, Sat. Closed Sun
Annual International Festival of the Sahara, Nov or Dec.
Camel treks organised by Douz Voyages 05 470178; Abdel Moulah Voyages 05 95484

Douz Museum
Avenue des Martyrs
8:30–1, 3–6 Mon–Sat
Cheap

GABÈS ✪✪

Initially Gabès appears to be a modern industrial city at the crossroads for tours to the interior, but it has more to offer. It was a major Phoenician and Roman port; during the 14th century it was on the main east–west trading route and was a transit stop for Muslim pilgrims en route to Mecca. It was heavily battered in World War II raids and by devastating floods in 1962 but the old town still has atmosphere with its *souq* and mosques, and its huge plantation of date palms is a true oasis.

28B4
405km south of Tunis
Wide choice of restaurants (£–££)
To Sfax, Sousse and Tunis
To Matmata
Avenue Hedi Chaker 05 270254

GAFSA ✪

A former Berber stronghold and a prosperous Roman town, Gafsa is an important regional centre and phosphate-producing town. Most tourists pass through on their way to the salt lakes and dunes but there is a picturesque *kasbah*, a huge date palm grove and the Piscines Romaines (Roman Pools) with a small museum.

28A4
93km northeast of Tozeur
Good choice (£–££)
To Tunis, Tozeur, Sfax
Place des Piscines Romaines 06 221664

28A4
16km west of Metlaoui
Le Lézard Rouge
Metlaoui station
06 241920; one departure a day
Expensive

Below: *this ancient underground dwelling at Matmata has been converted into a hotel*

GORGES DE SELJA ✪✪

This impressive 15km-long gorge stretches from Redeyef to Metlaoui, a thriving phosphate mining town. One of the best ways to see the gorge is from **Le Lézard Rouge** (the Red Lizard): a restored 19th-century train which operates a two-hour round-trip from Metlaoui. Selja itself is halfway along the gorge and is a good place to stop for a walk down into the deepest parts of the gorge. The railway tunnels and bridges were originally built by the French to transport phosphate from the mines to Gafsa (► 83).

KSAR OULED SOLTANE (► 22, TOP TEN)

28B3
43km southwest of Gabès
Up to ten buses a day to Gabès and daily services to Sfax, Sousse and Tunis
Main square 05 230114
Hôtel Marhala 05 230015, Hôtel Sidi Driss 05 230005, Hôtel Berbères 05 230024
By arrangement

MATMATA ✪✪✪

One of the best-known villages in Tunisia, mostly due to the opening sequence of the original *Star Wars* movie which featured its troglodyte dwellings. Dating from the fourth century BC, many of the underground houses are still inhabited, providing homes that are cool in summer and warm in winter. Some of the houses can be visited by arrangement with the owners, but it is advisable to arrange a price beforehand or buy some of the craft goods on sale. Three of the traditional dwellings in Old Matmata have been turned into hotels: the Marhala, part of a chain run by the Touring Club de Tunisie; the Hôtel Sidi Driss whose bar also appeared in the film as the setting for the alien jazz club sequence; and Les Berbères – named after the people who have lived here for centuries.

A whitewashed mosque stands alone in the desert near Midès

MIDÈS ✪✪

The oasis village of Midès is in the mountains which border Algeria. Originally a Berber village, Midès became an outpost of the Roman Empire. All but a handful of residents have now left their single room mud brick houses in the original village perched precariously on the sides of the deep gorge, and moved to the new town which has been built on the other side of the palm grove. The oasis itself is, as usual, a place of refuge from the fierce heat of this desert region. The Tunisian government is now helping to restore the old houses as tourist accommodation, and shops that sell local produce and souvenirs to a small but steadily increasing stream of day-trippers.

28A4
75km west of Gafsa
None; join an organised excursion or hire a car

DID YOU KNOW?

Sufism is a devout sect which has been marginalised by Orthodox Islam. Followers seek to achieve a direct relationship with God through spiritual association rather than by learning Koranic texts. They are known for achieving a trance-like state through chanting, dancing and meditation.

NEFTA ✪✪

The main attractions in Nefta are the Qasr El-Aïn (➤ 23, Top Ten) which is set in a deep basin (the Corbeille or 'basket') below the town, and the other oasis which lies just to the south. But Nefta itself is worth exploring too. The best-preserved of Nefta's Old Town districts is Ouled ech Cherif, where the narrow alleyways are often covered and the walls are decorated with traditional patterns created in the brickwork. There are literally dozens of mosques throughout the old quarters with Sidi M'Khareg in one of the most scenic positions overlooking the oasis.

Nefta is a centre of Sufism – a branch of Islam (➤ above) – and the town has over a hundred shrines (or *marabouts*), that make this city the holiest in Tunisia after Kairouan (➤ 20–1) . The Zaouia de Sidi Brahim is the headquarters of an important Sufi order.

28A4
25km west of Tozeur
Hôtel Marhala (£) avenue de l'Environment 06 430027
Six a day to Tozeur. Daily services to Kairouan and Sfax
Tozeur–Nefta airport (23 km) for flights to Tunis and Jerba
Avenue Habib Bourguiba 06 430236
Thursday is market day

QASR EL-AÏN, NEFTA(➤ 24, TOP TEN)

28C2
70km south of Tataouine
Daily from Tataouine
Cafés (£) on place de l'Indépendance

Above: *the mud-brick village of Tamerza is fast dissolving back into the landscape*

REMADA

Remada is Tunisia's southernmost town, beyond which there is nothing but desert, is dominated by the military, due to the proximity of the Libyan border. Centred on a little oasis where the Romans had a small fort, day-to-day life focuses on the shady place de l'Indépendance. Remada's most distinctive sight is on the southern edge of town – a 15-domed mud brick building once used as a slaughterhouse. Borg Bourguiba, 40km southwest of Remada, is where Habib Bourguiba (► 14) was held prisoner for a year in the early 1950s.

28A4
85km west of Gafsa
Tamerza Palace Hotel (££) 06 453844 Fax 06 453722
Two buses a day to Tunis and three a day to Gafsa
Tourist bureau Daily 8–6

TAMERZA

Once a Roman military post called Ad Turres, Tamerza later became the seat of a Christian bishop during the Byzantine era. The original village of Tamerza was devastated by catastrophic flooding in 1969 and now lies abandoned. Today visitors walk through its eerily empty streets; it looks strangely beautiful at night when floodlit and viewed from the comfort of the Tamerza Palace Hotel directly opposite. There is a small waterfall and a swimming area known as the Cascades.

28C3
49km south of Medenine
Hôtel Sangho (££) 3km from town on road to Chenini 05 860102 Fax 05 862177
To Sfax, Sousse and Tunis.
Festival of the Ksour, Apr

TATAOUINE

A good base for exploring the *ksour* or fortified villages (► 22, Top Ten). Tataouine is a Berber word meaning 'springs' and historically there was an important camel market here; there is still a busy market every Monday and Thursday held in and around the central *souq* – one of the best places to buy *kilims* (woven rugs) and pottery. Ksar Megabla, 2km south of the town centre, offers good views of the surrounding area.

Traditional brick designs adorn the entrance to the oasis in Tozeur

Tozeur

The area around Tozeur has been inhabited since at least 8000 BC, sited around an oasis on the northern shore of the great salt lake of Chott el Jerid (➤ 82). The town prospered as a trading post on the route of the great trans-Saharan caravans but today Tozeur is the focal point of Tunisia's ever-expanding desert tourist industry. Until relatively recently Tozeur was merely an overnight stop on desert safaris from the east coast resorts, but it is now an established resort in its own right.

28A4
220km west of Gabès; 450km south of Tunis
Good choice (£–£££) around avenue Bourguiba
To Tunis, Nefta, Gafsa and Kebili
Regular flights to Tunis, Djerba and Monastir
Avenue Abdul Kacem Chebbi ☎ 06 450503
Bedouin Festival, Dec

What to See in Tozeur

BELVÉDÈRE ✪

This rocky outcrop offers panoramic views over the palm grove (➤ 89), the Chott el Jerid (➤ 82) and the Chott el Gharsa. It is a 20-minute walk from the Dar Cheraït (➤ below); go early in the morning or at sunset, or at night when the site is floodlit.

3km southwest of the town centre
Open access
None
Free

DAR CHERAÏT MUSEUM ✪✪

Purpose-built in the style of an upper-class Tunis townhouse, the displays depict scenes from Tunisian life past and present: there is a typical kitchen, a *bey's* bedroom, a wedding scene, a *hammam* and a Bedouin tent. There are displays of costumes, jewellery, ceramics and sacred books; and the work of weavers, cobblers and tailors is also highlighted. A sound-and-light show called 'One Thousand and One Nights' is based (very) loosely on the book of the same name.

Route Touristique
06 452100
8AM–midnight
None
Moderate

A Walk Around Tozeur

Distance
5km

Time
Half a day allowing for visits

Start/end point
Grand Hôtel de l'Oasis
28A4
place des Martyrs
06 452699

Drinks
Cafés (£) on avenue Habib Bourguiba

This walk combines Tozeur's busy central thoroughfare with a glimpse of the palmery.

Start at the Grand Hôtel de l'Oasis and walk up avenue Habib Bourguiba.

Tozeur's main street is a curious mix of sleepy desert town catering for the everyday needs of local people and brash tourist centre with dozens of shops selling carpets, pottery and stuffed camels.

At the tiered pottery bowl landmark turn right for a look around Tozeur's covered market hall. Walk past the slim sandstone minaret of Mosquée El Farkous, turning right at the end of avenue Habib Bourguiba. Continue straight ahead at place des Martyrs. Take the second right towards Mosquée Sidi Abdesallem at the far end. Veer left towards a dome-shaped tiled monument in front of the École Primaire ibn Chabbat and walk down the left-hand side of the school. After 200m, at the end of a concrete wall, turn right following the path through a courtyard to the palmery.

Tozeur's palmery (► 89) covers around 10sq km, has more than 200,000 palm trees and 200 springs.

After two or three minutes' walk, cross a small stream, turn left out of the palmery and then right following a path leading into the médina. *Take the third turning right, under a double arch. Note the roofs made of dried palm trunks.*

Call in at the Musée des Arts et Traditions Populaires (► 89).

Turn right out of the museum. At the end of the street turn left which leads back to avenue Habib Bourguiba.

Tozeur's palmery is a lush oasis of greenery

MUSÉE DES ARTS ET TRADITIONS POPULAIRES (MUSEUM OF ARTS AND POPULAR TRADITIONS)

This museum illustrates traditional life with costumes, pottery and furniture. One of the most interesting exhibits is a collection of manuscripts describing Tozeur's water system. Originally conceived in the 13th century by the town's *imam* (religious leader) Ibn Chabbat, the distribution network was handed down orally from generation to generation until finally committed to paper in 1911.

Rue de Kairouan
8–6 Mon–Sat. 8–2:30 Sun
Cheap

OULED EL HADEF

Tozeur's Old Town is a web of narrow alleys which have changed little since the 14th century when it was built by the Ouled el Hadef tribe. Its distinctive architecture is considered to be one of the marvels of Islamic art. Unique to Tozeur and neighbouring Nefta (► 85), houses are decorated with geometric motifs (also found on local carpets and shawls). The yellowish bricks are handmade from a mix of local sand and clay, soaked in water, shaped in a wooden frame and left to dry in the sun before being baked in a kiln for three days. The bricks provide excellent insulation against the extremes of the desert climate, swelteringly hot in summer and freezing on winter nights.

North and east of the Hôtel Splendid
Choice of cafés (£)
Free

PALMERY

Within the oasis at Tozeur are thousands of date palms and hundreds of springs; the oasis is best viewed from the Belvédère (► 87), from a **hot air balloon**, or from a *calèche* (horse-drawn carriage) which you can hire to drive around the palm groves. A popular stop on every tourist circuit is the Paradis, a lush tropical garden which is seen at its best in early spring.

Northeast of the Market Square
Calèches for hire from opposite the Hôtel Karim
Open access
Free
Hot air balloon flights: Aeroasis
avenue Abdul Kacem Chabbi
06 452 361
Fax 06 451 500

The minaret of the Mosque El Farkous is built of thousands of tiny bricks arranged in geometric designs

Tozeur to Kebili: the road across the Chott

Distance
186km

Time
Allow five hours including time for lunch and a bathe in the Roman pool

Start/end point
Tozeur
28A4

Lunch
Hôtel l'Oasis dar Kebili (££–£££)
Zone Touristique de Kebili
05 491436

A drive along the causeway across the Chott El Jerid which can produce stunning mirages.

Leave Tozeur heading northeast on the GP3. After 8km drive through the village of Bouhel, turn right and 3km later pass through Degache, which marks the start of the 80km-long / 2m-high causeway across the Chott.

The Chott El Jerid (► 82) is one of a series of giant salt lakes that divide the north of the country from the true desert landscape of the south. There are no significant landmarks en route; however, look out for the abandoned burnt-out shell of a bus and a handful of isolated huts and stalls selling souvenirs. The terrain can appear to change enormously according to the time of year and the brightness of the sunshine. In winter if there has been quite a lot of rain it is not unusual for the water to look pink on one side of the road and green on the other; this is caused by the natural chemicals in the water.

The first signs of life come as you pass through the village of Souk Lahad, which is worth a short stop. You reach Kebili after another 15km.

Kebili was an important slave-trading town until the 19th century but is now simply a regional transport centre. There is a large palm grove, and just outside town – 1km south on the road to Douz – a Roman bathing pool and *hammam* fed by a 3km-deep borehole.

Leave Kebili, returning to Tozeur along the causeway.

The 90km-long causeway across the Chott el Jerid, the largest salt lake in southern Tunisia

Where To...

Eat and Drink	92–7
Stay	98–103
Shop	104–7
Take the Children	108–9
Be Entertained	110–16

Above: *Guellala pottery*
Right: *a character in* A Thousand and One Nights

Tunis & the North

Prices
The restaurants listed in this section have been grouped into three price categories based on a three-course meal per person without drinks.
£ = budget – less than 10D
££ = moderate – 15–25D
£££ = expensive – over 25D

Bizerte

Le Bonheur (£)
Grilled meats, fish and seafood at this simple but convivial local restaurant.
31 rue Thaalbi 02 431047 Lunch, dinner

L'Eden (££–£££)
Fresh fish and seafood specialities on a flower-adorned terrace 3km from the town centre.
route de la Corniche 02 439023 Lunch, dinner

Le Petit Mousse (££)
In hotel of the same name (➤ 100). The upstairs dining room offers a long French-inspired menu; in summer grilled fish and pizzas are served outside.
route de la Corniche 02 432185 Lunch, dinner

Le Sport Nautique (£££)
Seafront restaurant near town centre. Ideal for a leisurely lunch, with people-watching thrown in.
boulevard Habib Bougatfa 02 431495 Lunch, dinner

La Goulette

Le Café Vert (££)
The leader among the cluster of mid- to up-market fish restaurants. *Poisson Complet* is the most requested dish.
68 avenue Franklin Roosevelt 01 736156 Lunch, dinner

Lucullus (££)
This popular fish restaurant features uniformed waiters and tables set with linen tablecloths.
1 avenue Habib Bourguiba 01 737310 Lunch, dinner

Sidi Bou Saïd

Café des Nattes (£)
Allow time to linger and relax while enjoying a coffee at this atmospheric Moorish café overlooking Sidi Bou Saïd's main street.
place Sidi Bou Saïd All day

Café Sidi Chabanne (£)
Sit outside sipping the house speciality – mint tea sprinkled with pinenuts – while admiring the view of the Gulf of Tunis. You will pay well over the odds but, for once, it's worth it.
rue el Hadi Zarrouk All day

Tabarka

Hôtel de France (£)
The three-course set menu here represents good value, and as an added bonus you can have a beer with your meal.
avenue Habib Bourguiba 08 644 577 Lunch, dinner

Tunis

Le Baghdad (££–£££)
A rather formal restaurant with uniformed doorman. The Tunisian specialities are good and there is occasional evening cabaret.
29 avenue Bourguiba (next to the Carlton Hotel) 01 259 068 Lunch, dinner

Bolero (££)
This eaterie is located in a scruffy alley off rue de Yougoslavie, but is very popular with local residents. The main choice is between grilled meats and seafood – and there is a good value tourist menu.
passage el-Guattar 01 245 928 Lunch, dinner

Café de Paris (£)
Always busy and a convenient meeting place and people-watching spot. One of the few cafés to serve beer.
✉ corner of avenue Habib Bourguiba and avenue de Carthage ⌚ All day

Café Plantation (£)
Smiling, customer-friendly staff and a pleasant ambience make this a welcome addition to Tunis's café scene.
✉ 12–14 rue de Marseille ☎ 01 343565 ⌚ All day

Capitole Restaurant (££)
Long-established, reasonably priced first-floor restaurant with a particularly good tourist menu.
✉ 60 avenue Habib Bourguiba ☎ 01 256601 ⌚ Lunch, dinner

Chez Nous (££)
Photos of guests such as Edith Piaf and Muhammad Ali line the walls of this intimate French restaurant which offers good *à la carte* and set menus.
✉ 5 rue de Marseille ☎ 01 243048 ⌚ Lunch, dinner. Closed Sun and Ramadan

Le Cosmos (££)
The white-jacketed waiters don't make new customers feel welcome, possibly because the restaurant enjoys a strong local following. The food is good and the place has a certain old-fashioned charm.
✉ 7 rue ibn Khaldoun ☎ 01 241610 ⌚ Lunch, dinner. Closed Sun and Ramadan

Dar El Jeld (£££)
Said to be the best restaurant in Tunis and it certainly has a grand setting in the former mansion of a fabulously wealthy family. It provides superb Tunisian cooking with gracious service and discreet musical accompaniment. Advance booking recommended.
✉ rue Dar el Jeld ☎ 01 260916 ⌚ Lunch, dinner. Closed Sun

Gaston's (££)
Good value lunchtime tourist menu and a more extensive *à la carte* selection. Occasional live music.
✉ 73 rue de Yougoslavie ☎ 01 340417 ⌚ Lunch, dinner

Hollywood Dinners (££)
New movie-theme restaurant with some nice touches like presenting the bill in a metal filmreel case. The staff are welcoming but the food is over-fussy and lacks star quality.
✉ 12–14 rue de Marseille ☎ 01 343565 ⌚ Lunch, dinner

La Mamma (£)
Pizzas and pasta as well as a range of Tunisian dishes at this dependable Italian-style restaurant which draws a continual flow of regular customers.
✉ 11 rue de Marseille ☎ 01 241256 ⌚ Lunch, dinner

Les Margaritas (££)
Formal restaurant attached to the Hôtel Maison Dorée (► 101). Very popular as a lunchtime venue for local people. The set menu is good value.
✉ rue de Hollande ☎ 01 240631 ⌚ Lunch, dinner. Closed Sun

Grabbing a Sandwich
If you do not feel like having a full meal at lunchtime, drop in at a sandwich bar or pizzeria (both of which can be found all over Tunisia) and ask for a '*cassecroute*'. This is a thick chunk of French bread – usually buttered with fiery *harissa* sauce – then generously filled with lettuce, tomato, egg, tuna, olives and occasionally boiled potatoes or sausage.

Cap Bon

Self-help for Self-caterers

If you are on a self-catering holiday do not expect Tunisian supermarkets to be as well stocked as those in Europe or North America. Many food stores are part of larger shops selling a variety of household goods. The best advice is to shop Tunisian-style and buy food fresh from market stalls.

El Haouaria

L'Épervier (£–££)

Straightforward food at this popular venue busy with tour groups at lunchtime and a local crowd in the evening.
rue Hedi Chaker 02 297017 Lunch, dinner

Hammamet

Belle Vue (£–££)

Everything from soup and salads to full meals at this busy restaurant.
Centre Commercial, avenue Habib Bourguiba 02 280825 Lunch, dinner

Café Sidi Bou Hdid (£)

Also known as Café des Muriers. An atmospheric domed café which is at its best on warm summer evenings, when customers spill out on to the surrounding ramparts to sip coffee, smoke *chicas* and mull over the events of the day.
Seafront end of the *médina* All day

Le Carrefour (££)

Adjoining a popular bar run by three brothers. Pizza and fish highly recommended.
avenue des Nations Unies (outside the town centre close to the Hotel Miramar ➤ 102) 02 281776 Lunch, dinner

La Casa Doro (£££)

The extensive menu in five languages on boards outside suggests a cheap outlet but this is a place to linger over dinner, enjoying good food and attentive service.
60 avenue Habib Bourguiba 02 260099 Lunch, dinner

Chez Achour (££–£££)

Tucked away in a side street, this restaurant is solidly dependable with a strong local following and outside seating in summer. Fish is the house speciality.
rue Ali Belahouane, off avenue de la République 02 280140 Lunch, dinner

La Pergola (££)

Pleasant location with a large outside terrace awash with greenery. Efficient service and comprehensive menu with everything from soups and salads to grilled meats and fish.
Centre Commercial, avenue Habib Bourguiba 02 261750 Lunch, dinner

Pomodoro (££–£££)

The style of this restaurant is as discreet as its first floor location. A seriously classy but unstuffy place to eat, with courteous staff and excellent food.
avenue Habib Bourguiba 02 281254 Lunch, dinner

Restaurant Barberousse (££)

Hugely popular in the summer months with its roof terrace overlooking the *médina*. Both view and food are good value.
Entrance to the *médina* 02 280037 Lunch, dinner

Restaurant La Brise (£)

With its tiled floor and plastic tablecloths, this is not an ideal choice for dinner, but it is certainly worth considering for lunch, as its food is both wholesome and cheap.
2 avenue de la République 02 278910 Lunch, dinner

Restaurant Chinois (££)

For a change, try this

Chinese restaurant offering all the usual favourites.
Centre Commercial, avenue Habib Bourguiba 02 261937 Lunch, dinner

Restaurant Fatma (££)
Two minutes' walk from the *médina*. The service is pleasant but the food can be indifferent.
Commercial Centre, avenue Habib Bourguiba 02 280756 Lunch, dinner

RestoVert (£)
Cosy movie-themed café with walls lined with film posters. Serves simple food including salads and sandwiches.
avenue de la République All day

La Scala (£££)
The pasta is excellent at this intimate Italian restaurant themed around the La Scala Opera House in Milan. Book in advance.
off avenue des Nations Unies 02 287168 Lunch, dinner. Closed in winter

La Sirene (£–££)
Very casual beachfront restaurant/snack bar with shaded terrace. Wide range of food from pizzas and crêpes to grilled fish and *couscous*.
avenue Assad ibn el Fourat close to Hotel Belle Vue Lunch, dinner

Les Trois Moutons (££–£££)
One of the best restaurants in town, with excellent meat and fish dishes. Offers an extensive menu and a good value set dinner.
Centre Commercial, avenue Habib Bourguiba 02 280981 Lunch, dinner

Kélibia

Anis (£)
Very good value town centre budget restaurant offering Tunisian specialities and pleasant service.
avenue Erriadh 02 295777 Lunch, dinner

Restaurant El-Mansourah (££)
Choose grilled fish and salad with a bottle of the local Muscat de Kélibia, a refreshing medium-dry white wine.
Out beyond Kélibia's fort, at the southern end of Mansourah Beach 02 295169 Lunch, dinner

Nabeul

Café Errachida (£)
A welcoming café specialising in mint tea served with tempting sticky cakes.
avenue Habib Thameur (at the junction with avenue Habib Bourguiba) All day

Restaurant Bon Kif (££–£££)
Attracts as many local diners as it does tourists; ideal for a long, lazy lunch or dinner. Excellent grilled fish and succulent seafood, matched with quietly efficient service and Tunisian décor.
avenue Marbella (off avenue Habib Thameur) 02 222783 Lunch, dinner

Restaurant de l'Olivier (£££)
This restaurant is not cheap, but it offers up-market French cooking in smart surroundings. The wine list includes imported wines as well as some that have been produced locally.
6 avenue Hedi Chaker Lunch, dinner

Time for Tea?
Although mint tea is Tunisia's national drink, standards can vary enormously. Outside the main tourist areas many cafés serve a very sweet lukewarm mixture of gunpowder tea and sugar – often well stewed. For a piping hot glass of freshly-brewed mint tea topped with pinenuts it would be hard to better the Café Sidi Chabanne in Sidi Bou Saïd (► 92).

Central Tunisia

Rôtisseries and Gargottes
Rôtisseries are the cheapest of Tunisia's restaurants. Aimed at working men, they are easily identified by a rotating spit of roasting chickens at the entrance. This is usually the only food served – accompanied by chips and salad. Gargottes offer a wider range of food including *chorba* (spicy soup), kebabs and *merguez* sausages, but still served in very basic surroundings.

Iles Kerkennah

La Sirène (££)
Looks like a glorified beach hut, but serves excellent fresh fish and seafood. Friendly service and good value. In the summer you can sit out on a shaded terrace overlooking the sea and have a beer.
On the beachfront at the end of the road next to Hôtel el-Jazira in Remla 04 481118 Lunch, dinner

Le Kef

Vénus (££)
One of the best restaurants in town, offering good value set price meals and an extensive *à la carte* choice.
rue Farhat Hached 08 200355 Lunch, dinner

Mahdia

Le Lido (££–£££)
Brightly lit, Le Lido draws a good mix of tourists and locals. Opposite the fishing port, fish *couscous* is a favourite here, as well as grilled fish and seafood.
avenue Farhat Hached 03 681339 Lunch, dinner

Restaurant el-Moez (£)
Popular with local people; fish soup and *kammounia* are among the specialities served here.
In a small side street between Skifa el Kahla and rue des Fatmides Lunch, dinner

Monastir

La Plage (£)
Dine overlooking the sea at this restaurant close to the fishing port; naturally, fresh fish is the speciality of the house.
place du 3 Août 03 461124 Lunch, dinner

Les Remparts (£–££)
Concentrates on pizzas during the day, but offers a more extensive menu in the evenings. Service is a little slow, but if you are sitting outside watching the world go by it does not matter too much.
avenue Habib Bourguiba 03 460752 Lunch, dinner

Roi du Couscous (£)
Cheap, cheerful and popular, with outside seating. Some may be deterred by the swarm of cats waiting to be thrown titbits.
place du Gouvernorate Lunch, dinner

Port El Kantaoui

La Daurade (££–£££)
Fresh fish tops the menu at this popular venue with outdoor seating in demand at lunch and dinner. Worth booking ahead to secure one of the best tables.
The Marina 03 244893 Lunch, dinner

Sfax

Café Diwan (£)
A popular café with a rooftop terrace offering views over the city wall. A quiet, relaxed place to stop for tea or coffee during the day or to mingle with local people in the evenings.
off rue de la Kasbah, next to No 37 8 till late

Chez Nous (££)
The food here is good, even if the service is somewhat surly. Tunisian specialities include various *ojjas* (egg dishes) and fish *couscous*.
26 rue Patrice Lumumba 04 227128 Lunch, dinner

Le Corail (£££)
Rather formal but no complaints about the food.
39 rue Habib Mazoun 04 227301 Lunch, dinner

La Gondole (£)
Pocket-sized daytime café with a handful of seats and constantly changing flow of customers. Good for coffee and croissants; the window seat is well-placed for people watching.
Taieb M'Hiri 7AM–8PM

Mamma Rosa (£)
Good quality pizza and pasta, friendly staff and attentive service.
55 avenue Farhat Hached 04 225886 Lunch, dinner

Le Printemps (££)
Despite its smart appearance the food and service are a bit disappointing. Stick to the set menu.
55 avenue Habib Bourguiba 04 226973 Lunch, dinner

Sousse

La Calèche (£££)
Aimed squarely at the tourist market but most dishes are quite pricey. Set menu is good value.
rue Remada 03 226489 Lunch, dinner

Hong Kong Restaurant (£££)
Here is an alternative to *briks* and *couscous* but the *à la carte* selection is quite expensive. The set menu is better value.
boulevard de Rabat – opposite El Hana Beach Hotel 03 221366 Lunch, dinner

Le Lido (££)
A restaurant in a great location opposite the port, offering some outside seating. The menu is dominated by excellent fresh fish.
avenue Mohammed V 03 225329 Lunch, dinner

El Pescador (£££)
A very good fish restaurant with seafood pasta among the specialities.
rue de Ribat 03 226260 Lunch, dinner. Closed Mon

Restaurant Les Remparts (££)
This atmospheric restaurant is located next to the Hôtel de Tunis and just inside the walls of the *médina*.
17 rue de l'Église 03 226326 Lunch, dinner

Les Sportifs (££)
A popular venue, endorsed by several European tour operators. Good food and service at value-for-money prices.
avenue Bourguiba 03 224756 Lunch, dinner

Tip Top (££)
Aimed at the holiday market, Tip Top is a deservedly popular choice, offering a warm welcome, cosy ambience and excellent choice of food.
boulevard de la Corniche 03 226158 Lunch, dinner

Restaurant Le Viking (£££)
Centrally placed off avenue Bourguiba, Le Viking can be expensive so it's best to stick to the set menus.
rue de l'Algerie 03 228377 Lunch, dinner

Blowing Bubbles
In most bars there will be several men smoking *chichas* – also known as hookah pipes. This is the most popular way of smoking in Tunisia. Contrary to popular perception, the water pipes are not filled with hashish but with *tombac*, a close relative of tobacco. The *tombac* is placed on top of the pipe and covered with a very hot piece of charcoal. The smoke is then filtered through the water before being inhaled.

Jerba & the South

Tipping and TGV

Waiters do not expect to be tipped in the same way as they do in Europe and North America. In budget restaurants it is acceptable to leave a few coins unless the food and service were exceptional, in which case you may wish to leave more. In tourist restaurants it is more normal to leave ten per cent – but only if the service merits it. Always check to see if service has already been included. TGV is not the service charge but a sales tax.

Gabès

Restaurant el Mazar (£££)

Despite its name this is basically a good French restaurant with Tunisian influences.

39 avenue Farhat Hached 05 272065 Lunch, dinner

Restaurant de l'Oasis (£££)

Generally reckoned to be the top spot in Gabès. The set menu is good value.

17 avenue Farhat Hached 05 270098 Lunch, dinner

Jerba

Aladin (£)

Fish and some interesting seafood dishes at this small, low-priced restaurant.

40 avenue Mohamed Badra, Houmt Souq Lunch, dinner

Baccar (££)

Split-level tourist-oriented restaurant offering all the usual Tunisian specialities including various types of *couscous*.

place Hedi Chaker, Houmt Souq 05 650708 Lunch, dinner

Blue Moon (££–£££)

Stylish and spacious air-conditioned restaurant heavily geared to tourists with a good value set menu and much more expensive *à la carte* selection.

place Hedi Chaker, Houmt Souq 05 650559 Lunch, dinner

Dar Faïza (£)

Good value set price menu in a cosy hotel dining room where it can be hard to find a table in high season.

rue de la République, Houmt Souq 05 650083 Fax 05 651763 Dinner

El Hana (££–£££)

Dine by candlelight with linen napkins and tablecloths at this snug, welcoming little restaurant which feels like someone's front room. The food is very good with exceptional mashed potato dishes.

place 7 Novembre, Houmt Souq 05 650568 Dinner

La Mamma (£)

You can eat with the locals at this atmospheric and cheap eatery which does a roaring trade in soups and *couscous*.

rue Habib Bourguiba, Houmt Souq All day

Les Palmiers (£)

Come to this friendly restaurant for great value eating. With its colourful menu, pretty tablecloths, pictures on the wall and subtle lighting it is a cut above most Tunisian budget restaurants and worth a visit. No alcohol is permitted.

place d'Algerie, Houmt Souq Lunch, dinner

La Princesse d'Haroun (£££)

Jerba's most famous restaurant. In summer you can eat on the terrace overlooking the harbour. Meat dishes available but seafood starters and grilled fish rule the waves. Smart casual dress preferred.

Opposite the fishing harbour 05 650488 Lunch, dinner

Restaurant de l'Ile (££–£££)

This is a rather formal, serious restaurant, and quite pricey; the set menu represents the best value.

off place Hedi Chaker, Houmt Souq 05 650651 Lunch, dinner

Restaurant du Sportif (£–££)
Starkly lit restaurant catering for a mainly local clientele mostly with meat grills and stews.
147 avenue Habib Bourguiba 11–9

Restaurant du Sud (££–£££)
Aimed squarely at the tourist trade but with better food than most.
off place Hedi Chaker 05 650479 Lunch, dinner

Tamerza

Tamerza Palace Hotel (££)
Good for lunch or dinner with agreeable food, attentive service and excellent views of the abandoned village of Tamerza.
Tamerza 06 453722 Fax 06 799910

Tozeur

La Diamanta (£)
Not a place to linger but perfectly good for a quick lunch or light supper. No alcohol.
avenue Abou El Kacem Chabbi 06 453867

L'Grand Oasis (££)
The three-course evening buffet is good value but get there early while the food is fresh and hot.
avenue Abou el Kacem Chabbi 06 452699 Dinner

Le Palmeraie (£££)
An expensive but pleasant hotel restaurant offering high standards of food and service. A tourist menu is available.
Hotel Palmeraie 06 452041 Lunch, dinner

Le Petit Prince (££)
Long-established restaurant which sometimes has evening shows of traditional music and dancing.
off avenue Abou el Kacem Chabbi leading into the palmery 06 450097 Dinner

Restaurant de la République (£)
Tucked away in a corner, this cosy little restaurant appeals to local people and tourists. Good, affordable food.
avenue Habib Bourguiba (on the west side at the back of an arcade of shops) Lunch, dinner

Restaurant Sheherezad (£££)
Part of the Dar Charait complex. Good food and gracious surroundings.
Zone Touristique 06 452100 Dinner

Restaurant du Sud (£)
Basic restaurant very popular with young travellers, serving a range of Tunisian specialities at rock bottom prices.
avenue Farhat Hached (opposite Agil petrol station) 06 450826 Lunch, dinner

Le Soleil (£)
Opposite Résidence Warda, the best of Tozeur's budget options with clean surroundings and an extensive menu. Camel-meat *couscous* is available if ordered in advance.
avenue Abou Kacem el Chabbi 06 554220 Lunch, dinner

Hot-Headed
Harissa can be a bit of a shock to the system on first acquaintance but many visitors develop such a liking for the fiery hot chilli paste that they take home a jar or two at the end of their trip. Used throughout the countries of the Maghreb for soups, stews and *couscous*, it is made up from ground dried red chilli peppers, garlic, coriander, cumin seeds, sea salt and olive oil.

Tunis & the North

Prices
The hotels listed are grouped into three categories based on one night's double room in high season including breakfast and taxes. All rooms have en suite facilities unless otherwise stated.
£ = budget – under 30D
£££ = expensive – over 80D
££ = moderate – 30D-80D

Bizerte

Abou Nawas Gammarth (£££)
Luxury hotel with a Moorish café and Tunisian/Moroccan restaurant convenient for Tunis Airport and the ruins of Carthage.
⊠ 20km north of Tunis, 10km from the airport ☎ 01 741444 Fax 01 740400

Bizerta Resort (£££)
Beachfront hotel in the *Zone Touristique* with indoor and outdoor swimming pools and a health club. The bedrooms are equipped with minibars and satellite television.
⊠ route de la Corniche ☎ 02 436966 Fax 02 422955

La Résidence (£££)
One of Tunisia's newest and most luxurious hotels with a thalassotherapy spa, tennis courts, Mediterranean restaurant and free shuttle service to Tunis city centre.
⊠ 2km north of Gammarth ☎ 01 910101 Fax 01 749888

Le Petit Mousse (££)
Well-run hotel with an excellent restaurant (➤ 92). One of its few negative features is that the private beach is just a very narrow strip, close to the road.
⊠ route de la Corniche ☎ 02 432185 Fax 02 437595

Sidi Bou Saïd

Dar Said (££)
Small attractive hotel, often recommended as a good choice for honeymooners.
⊠ Top of the main street ☎ 01 740471 Fax 01 256908

Dar Zarrouk (£££)
A recently renovated former palace, the Dar Zarrouk is right in the heart of Sidi bou Saïd and must be booked well in advance. The courtyard garden is a haven of peace and quiet.
⊠ rue el Hadi Zarrouk ⊠ 01 740591

Sidi Bou Saïd (£££)
This small recently renovated hotel is owned by the Tunisian National Tourist Office to provide hands-on experience for students at the adjacent hotel school. Full of character, it has a swimming pool, tennis courts and – from its sun terrace – an excellent view of Tunis.
⊠ avenue Sidi Dhrif (800m north of the village) ☎ 01 740411 Fax 01 745129

Tabarka

Abou Nawas Montazah (£££)
This sprawling beachfront hotel boasts five tennis courts and a diving centre – but the rooms can be very noisy.
⊠ route Touristique ☎ 08 643532 Fax 08 643726

Hôtel De France (£)
Fairly basic town centre hotel with shared bathrooms; busy restaurant (➤ 92) and convivial bar. Habib Bourguiba stayed here in 1952 during his internal exile.
⊠ avenue Habib Bourguiba ☎ 08 644577

Royal Golf (£££)
Operates as an all-inclusive hotel in the summer with all meals, drinks, activities and entertainment included in the room rate. Aimed principally at tour groups.
⊠ route Touristique (2km from town centre) ☎ 08 673399 Fax 08 673838

Tunis

Abou Nawas (£££)
Located next to the Palais du Congres and within walking distance of the *médina*, this is one of Tunis's top hotels. It houses a high-class Italian restaurant, a fitness centre and a swimming pool.
✉ **avenue Mohammed V**
☎ **01 350355 Fax 01 352882**

L'Africa Méridien (£££)
One of the city's major landmarks and meeting points (► 30), L'Africa Méridien is conveniently situated fronting the bustling main thoroughfare, a ten-minute walk from the *médina*. The hotel's facilities are more modern than its drab, ugly exterior might suggest.
✉ **50 avenue Habib Bourguiba**
☎ **01 347477 Fax 01 347432**

Carlton (££)
A clean, central mid-market hotel, but lacking in a certain warmth both in the starkness of the rooms and the attitude of the staff.
✉ **31 avenue Habib Bourguiba**
☎ **01 330644 Fax 01 338168**

Excel (££)
A centrally located, clean and comfortable hotel, offering in-room television and telephone and a friendly bar.
✉ **35 avenue Habib Bourguiba**
☎ **01 355088 Fax 01 341929**

Hilton (£££)
Located near Parc du Belvédère and aimed at business travellers on expense accounts. Free shuttle services to the city centre and airport.
✉ **avenue de la Ligue Arabe**
☎ **01 782800 Fax 01 782208**

Maison Dorée (£–££)
A well-maintained budget hotel with luxurious bedding and the atmosphere of a bygone age. The staff are a little formal and unless you particularly like the sound of trams thundering past your window every few minutes ask for a room at the front of the hotel.
✉ **6 rue de Hollande (entrance in rue el Koufa)** ☎ **01 240632 Fax 01 332401**

Majestic (££)
One of the great old-established hotels of Tunis, but now beginning to show its age.
✉ **36 avenue de Paris** ☎ **01 332666 Fax 01 336908**

Médina (£)
Probably the most pleasant of the Old Town hotels with clean double rooms; however, there are no singles or en-suite facilities.
✉ **place de la Victoire** ☎ **01 255056**

Rue de Russie
Spotless hotel discreetly located in a back street just off the bustling rue el Jazira.
✉ **18 rue de Russie** ☎ **01 328883 Fax 01 321685**

Salammbo (£)
Very basic hotel with few en-suite facilities. Reasonably clean, but with an unwelcoming atmosphere.
✉ **6 rue de Grèce** ☎ **01 334252**

Transatlantique (£)
Another fairly basic hotel with large and noisy bedrooms, but attractively tiled lobby and passageways.
✉ **106 rue de Yougoslavie**
☎ **01 240680**

Bargain Beds
Outside the peak summer months the price of beds comes right down, often to half the high season rate. Hotel prices are fixed by the Ministry of Tourism and are usually displayed in hotel reception areas. Always agree on the rate in advance and ask to see the room before making up your mind.

Cap Bon

Tourist Terrain
Tunisia is very fond of its *zone touristiques* (tourist areas) where most big holiday hotels are located. They are often sited along some of the best stretches of beach, but they are usually also several kilometres from the heart of a town and so lack local flavour. They also give the impression that the Tunisian authorities want to keep tourists and local people apart – which rather defeats the object of visiting someone else's country.

Hammamet

Alya (££)
Excellent little place in the heart of Hammamet. The clean, comfortable rooms have en-suite showers with plenty of hot water. Back-facing rooms also have balconies with views across to the *médina*.
30 rue Ali Belhouane 02 280218 Fax 02 282365

Aziza (£££)
A family-oriented beachfront hotel which is very popular with tour groups. It includes a health club, tennis courts and disco.
boulevard Assad ibn el Fourat (3km from town centre) 02 283666 Fax 02 283099

Bel Azur (£££)
A Moorish-style hotel on a small headland with pretty gardens and two sandy beaches. There is a separate children's pool as well as a pizzeria, snack bar and an *à la carte* restaurant.
boulevard Assad ibn el Fourat (2km from town centre) 02 280544 Fax 02 280275

Belle Vue (££)
The advantage of this hotel is its superb beachfront location just 400m from the *médina*. All rooms are doubles; the hotel includes a billiard room and TV lounge.
boulevard Assad ibn el Fourat 02 281121 Fax 02 283156

Dar Hayet (£££)
The smallest and most discreet of Hammamet's deluxe hotels. Rooms are all doubles and are plushly decorated with locally produced furnishings; most have sea views. There is a pool, and a small café.
rue de la Corniche 02 283399 Fax 02 280424

Khella (££)
Town centre hotel within two minutes' walk of several restaurants. Clean and comfortable.
avenue de la République 02 283900 Fax 02 283704

Miramar (£££)
The hotel is well maintained and sits on a pleasantly uncrowded strip of beach. Shops and restaurants just across the road.
rue des Hôtels (4km from the centre) 02 280344 Fax 02 280586

Les Orangers (£££)
This two-hotel complex is some way out of the town centre. It offers a sandy beach, colourful gardens, a health club and a regular programme of evening entertainment.
route Touristique 02 280457 Fax 02 281077

La Résidence (£££)
One of Hammamet's longest-established tourist hotels and still one of the best. All rooms sleep up to four and have mini-kitchens. There is a rooftop terrace with swimming pool and a private beach; very close to the *médina*.
avenue Habib Bourguiba 02 280733 Fax 02 280396

Royal Azur (£££)
Every comfort at the best luxury hotel in Hammamet. Most rooms have sea views. Fully equipped spa uses seawater, mud and algae for health/beauty treatments.

✉ boulevard Assad ibn el Fourat (2km from town centre) ☎ 02 278500 Fax 02 278999

Sahbi (££)
Sprawling town centre hotel with a carpet bazaar taking up most of the ground and first floors. Spacious bedrooms decorated in Tunisian style.
✉ avenue de la République ☎ 02 280807 Fax 02 280134

Shératon (£££)
An extensive resort hotel with rooms built in small clusters in lush gardens. There are six tennis courts, a swimming pool and children's play area.
✉ route Touristique Hammamet Sud (6km from town centre) ☎ 02 226555 Fax 02 227301

Yasmina (£££)
Overlooking the town's main beach, surrounded by greenery and with excellent view of the *kasbah*. Sun terrace, swimming pool and paddling pool; pizzeria with outdoor seating and a miniature golf course.
✉ avenue Habib Bourguiba ☎ 02 280222 Fax 02 280593

El Haouaria

L'Épervier (££)
Situated off the main street and built round a pretty courtyard with jasmine and orange trees. A clean and comfortable hotel with almost the only restaurant in town.
✉ avenue Habib Bourguiba ☎ 02 297017 Fax 02 297258

Kelibia

Palmarina (££)
Newish hotel with swimming pool, café/bar and restaurant. The sun terrace overlooks a small beach and the colourful fishing harbour. Friendly, helpful staff.
✉ avenue des Martyrs ☎ 02 274062 Fax 02 274055

Nabeul

Hôtel Lido (£££)
A large complex with cottages in the grounds as well as the main hotel building. Every facility you would expect from a popular package destination.
✉ 3km east of Nabeul ☎ 02 285135 Fax 02 285487

Les Jasmins (££)
In a secluded tree-lined road five minutes' walk from a quiet beach. Popular with tour groups in summer, independent guests are still welcomed. Rooms are in two-storey blocks in gardens. Swimming pool and up-market seafood restaurant.
✉ rue Abou el Kacem Chabbi (just outside Nabeul town centre) ☎ 02 285343 Fax 02 285073

Khéops (£££)
This hotel caters mainly for a mix of well-heeled business travellers and European tour groups.
✉ avenue Mohamed V ☎ 02 286555 Fax 02 286024

Pension Les Oliviers (£–££)
A cut above average guesthouse with clean rooms and en-suite bathrooms in a large modern house surrounded by olive and citrus trees. Close to the beach and a minute's walk from the Hôtel Les Jasmins (► above).
✉ 11 rue de Havane ☎ 02 286865 ⊗ Closed in winter

Don't be Star-Struck
Do not pay too much attention to hotel star ratings as they can be very unreliable. Introduced some years ago, the star system was only ever intended to grade the physical facilities of a hotel – ignoring the quality of service offered altogether. Now, even the assessing of facilities seems somewhat lax.

Central Tunisia

Food for Thought
Avoid beach resort hotels which insist that you book half- or full-board. Hotels find this a useful way to boost their income, but for guests it can mean an endless round of rather bland 'international-style' buffets. It is far more interesting and adventurous to eat out – and frequently cheaper as well.

Iles Kerkennah

Grand (££)
Recently refurbished secluded beachfront hotel with swimming pool and tennis courts. Cycling and horse-riding available nearby.
✉ Sidi Frej ☎ 04 281267 Fax 04 281485

Jazira (£)
Small family-run hotel in the Old Town district of Mahdia.
✉ Er Remla ☎ 04 281058

Kairouan

Splendid (££)
Probably Kairouan's classiest hotel – although it has seen better days. The big rooms are clean and comfortable and have private bathrooms. Bar and licensed restaurant.
✉ rue 9 April (off avenue de la République) ☎ 07 227522 Fax 07 230829

Mahdia

Corniche (£)
Good value, small modern hotel about 2km west of the town centre.
✉ avenue 7 Novembre (just before Zone Touristique) ☎ 03 694201

Melia El Mouradi (£££)
Newish and fairly typical beachfront hotel aimed squarely at the package tourist market. Indoor and outdoor swimming pools, tennis courts and a nightclub.
✉ Zone Touristique ☎ 03 692111 Fax 03 692120

Monastir

Yasmine (£–££)
Family-run pension with single and double rooms and a licensed restaurant.
✉ route de la Falaise ☎ 03 462511

Port El Kantaoui

El Hana Hannibal Palace (£££)
One of Port El Kantaoui's longest-established hotels just a short stroll from the marina. Pleasant ambience with a popular lunchtime terrace restaurant.
☎ 03 348577 Fax 03 348321

Sfax

Abou Nawas (£££)
This well-located hotel, mainly aimed at business travellers, could do with sharpening up all round, from its dreary décor to its sluggish service.
✉ avenue Habib Bourguiba ☎ 04 225700 Fax 04 235960

Alexandre (£)
Very good value at this elegant old colonial-style building with enormous baths.
✉ 21 rue Alexandre Dumas ☎ 04 221911

De la Médina (£)
Cheap, cheerful but clean hotel in the *médina*. Shared bathrooms.
✉ 53 rue Mongi Slim ☎ 04 220354

La Paix (£)
Fairly basic hotel. Although rooms have showers, you have to be a bit of a contortionist to use them.
✉ 17 rue Alexandre Dumas ☎ 04 296437

Sousse

Abou Nawas Boujafaar (£££)
A mix of business travellers and holidaymakers at this plush beachfront hotel which is equally well placed for shopping and eating out. Facilities include a couple of

popular bars, a terrace restaurant and a thalassotherapy spa.
✉ **avenue Habib Bourguiba**
☎ **03 226030 Fax 03 226595**

Amira
Atmospheric *médina* hotel. All rooms have bath or shower and toilet. Staff are friendly and helpful. Breakfast is served on a rooftop terrace.
✉ **52 rue de France** ☎ **03 226325**

Claridge (£)
Once the most superior place in town, now overshadowed by the string of beach hotels along the corniche. Plenty of character and a central location between the *médina* and the beach. The large comfortable rooms all have a bath or shower – but not all have en suite toilets.
✉ **10 avenue Habib Bourguiba**
☎ **03 224759 Fax 03 227277**

El Hana Beach (£££)
A popular family hotel in colourful gardens. Guests can use the facilities of two neighbouring hotels: the El Hana and the Chems El Hana.
✉ **boulevard de la Corniche**
☎ **03 226900 Fax 03 226076**

Ennasim (££)
Bed and breakfast only but well placed for restaurants and just 100m from the beach.
✉ **boulevard de la Corniche**
☎ **03 227100 Fax 03 224488**

Farès (££)
Busy city centre hotel next to the railway station. All rooms have bathrooms and balconies.
✉ **boulevard Hassouna Ayachi**
☎ **03 227800 Fax 03 227380**

Hadrumète (£–££)
A once-flourishing two-star hotel which has fallen behind the times. Close to the port, it still retains plenty of character. Ask for a room with a balcony and enjoy the hotel's faded glory.
✉ **place Assad ibn el Fourat**
☎ **03 226291 Fax 02 226863**

Jawhara (££)
Situated right on the beach and with good facilities.
✉ **boulevard 7 Novembre** ☎ **03 225611 Fax 03 224123**

Médina (£)
One of the best hotels in the *médina*. Rooms have en suite bathrooms and open on to a small courtyard.
✉ **15 rue Othman Osman** ☎ **03 221722**

Paris (£)
Beautifully maintained budget hotel just inside the walls of the *médina*. Friendly management, lots of atmosphere – but shared washing facilities!
✉ **15 rue Rempart Nord** ☎ **03 220564 Fax 03 219038**

Sousse Azur (££)
Friendly, comfortable, close to the beach and good value for money.
✉ **5 rue Amilcar** ☎ **03 226960 Fax 03 228145**

Tej Mahaba (£££)
A massive 700-bed hotel, 200m from the beach in large gardens with indoor and outdoor pools, tennis courts, Turkish bath and seafood restaurant.
✉ **avenue Taieb Mehiri**
☎ **03 229800 Fax 03 229815**

Women Travellers
Finding somewhere to stay presents extra problems for women travellers, whether holidaying alone or in pairs. Cultural differences mean that western women can face a certain amount of pestering although serious threats are rare. The best advice is generally to avoid small *médina* hotels and stay in family-run pensions or major tourist hotels instead.

Jerba & the South

Marhalas
The Touring Club de Tunisie runs a chain of cheap, traditional hotels known as *marhalas*. Priced slightly higher than youth hostels, they offer basic but clean rooms and a warm welcome. The most popular *marhalas* include the one in Houmt Souq and the underground hotel at Matmata.

Douz

Mouradi (££)
Indoor and outdoor pools, a gym and *hammam* at this newest of the *Zone Touristique* hotels.
✉ Zone Touristique ☎ 05 470303 Fax 05 470905

Sun Palm Hotel (££)
Atmospheric mid-market hotel attracting a mix of Tunisians and tourists. Rooms are comfortable if rather sparse and service is very casual.
☎ 05 475123 Fax 05 470525

Gabès

Atlantic (£)
Once-grand colonial-style hotel long past its best, but still with some character.
✉ 4 avenue Habib Bourguiba ☎ 05 220034 Fax 05 221358

Chems (££)
Enormous beachfront bungalow complex with single and double rooms.
✉ On the beach ☎ 05 270547 Fax 05 274485

Jerba

Dar Faïza (££)
A popular family-run hotel on the beachfront road near the harbour. Rooms are basic but spotless with crisp white sheets; huge baths with plenty of hot water. There is a small pool in the garden, a bar and good restaurant open to non-residents (► 98).
✉ rue de la République ☎ 05 650083 Fax 05 651763

Erriadh (£)
This delightful *fondouk* (► panel, 107) in the heart of Houmt Souq oozes charm and character. Built around a vine-covered courtyard, rooms are prettily tiled and have en suite facilities.
✉ 10 rue Mohamed Ferjani ☎ 05 650756 Fax 05 650487

Jerba Beach (£££)
Built in traditional Tunisian style with windsurfing and waterskiing facilities, a swimming pool, fitness centre and tennis courts.
✉ Zone Touristique (13km from Houmt Souq) ☎ 05 657200 Fax 05 657357

Lotos (£–££)
Very spacious rooms, many with large balconies overlooking the coast.
✉ rue de la République ☎ 05 650026 Fax 05 651763

Marhala (£)
One of several character budget hotels run by the Touring Club de Tunisie (► panel). Small and basic rooms but loads of atmosphere and a busy bar.
✉ 13 rue Moncef Bey ☎ 05 650146 Fax 05 653317

Sables d'Or (£)
Converted house with a central patio in the centre of Houmt Souq. The 12 rooms are kept spotlessly clean and all have showers – but there are communal toilets.
✉ 30 rue Mohammed Ferjani ☎ 05 650423

Ulysse Palace (£££)
Beachfront hotel with several restaurants, a thalassotherapy spa and minibars and satellite television in all rooms.
✉ Zone Touristique ☎ 05 657422 Fax 05 757850

Matmata

Marhala (£)
This converted underground

house is run by the Touring Club de Tunisie (► panel). Popular, so book well ahead.
✉ **off Toujane road** ☎ **05 230015**

Nefta

Marhala (£-££)

This former brick factory on the edge of Nefta's oasis is now a hotel run by the Touring Club de Tunisie. Comfortable and friendly, it has recently opened a new wing and swimming pool.
✉ **route Touristique** ☎ **06 430027 Fax 06 430511**

Rose (£££)

Block-booked by mainly German tour groups in the peak summer season, this comfortable hotel is often almost empty in winter when room rates take a dramatic dive.
✉ **route Touristique** ☎ **06 430697 Fax 06 430385**

Tamerza

Tamerza Palace Hotel (££–£££)

Stylish, well-run hotel overlooking the ruined village of Tamerza. A good base for exploring the desert region.
☎ **06 453722 Fax 06 799910**

Tozeur

Abou Nawas (£££)

Palatial hotel on the edge of the palm grove with an elegant marble-floored lobby with gushing fountain. Bedrooms are in two-storey blocks in the gardens. French speciality restaurant or a gloomy cafeteria.
✉ **route Touristique** ☎ **06 453500 Fax 06 452686**

Basma (£££)

Over-priced tourist hotel very popular with French tour groups. Attractive bar and lobby area. Dull bedrooms.
✉ **route Touristique** ☎ **06 452488 Fax 06 452294**

Continental (££)

Long-established mid-market hotel on the edge of the palm grove with comfortable rooms and a swimming pool.
✉ **avenue Aboul Kacem Chebbi** ☎ **06 461411 Fax 06 452109**

Grand Oasis (££)

Popular hotel with tourists on desert safaris. The rooms are a bit like cells but the service is friendly and there is a decent bar and restaurant.
✉ **avenue Aboul Kacem Chebbi** ☎ **06 450522 Fax 06 452153**

Palm Beach (£££)

The most expensive hotel in Tozeur. This was where the cast of *The English Patient* stayed when filming in the desert. Every comfort provided including a luxurious spa.
✉ **route Touristique** ☎ **06 453111 Fax 06 453911**

Palmeraie (£££)

An upmarket hotel which offers a genuine touch of style and class. Plush bedrooms, a spacious lobby, decent restaurant, swimming pool and gardens backing on to the palm grove. Worth the price.
✉ **route Touristique** ☎ **06 454599 Fax 06 454833**

Résidence Warda (£)

Very basic rooms with en suite showers and scorching hot water.
✉ **avenue Abdel Kacem Chabbi** ☎ **06 452597**

Fondouks

Similar to *marhalas* in offering simple accommodation at cheap prices, *fondouk* hotels – of which there are several in Jerba – have all been built round old courtyards. Originally these would have been used for stabling horses and storing goods while merchants lived in rooms above. *Fondouk* hotels are some of the most atmospheric in Tunisia and well worth a night or two's stay.

Shopping in Tunisia

Hassle...

Do not expect to be allowed to shop in peace in Tunisia. There is little understanding – or desire to understand – the concept of browsing. Enter a tourist shop and an 'assistant' will immediately shadow your every move continuously pointing out the obvious, informing you very graciously that there is 'no charge for looking' and seizing upon even a slight flicker of interest in any item.

Markets

No trip to Tunisia would be complete without at least one visit to a local market. Outside the main towns they are the driving force and economic hub of rural communities. Lives are planned around the event: it is not only where all purchases are made for the week ahead but is a chance to see friends and catch up on local gossip. Tunisian markets are noisy, bustling and colourful and – even if you are not planning to buy anything – they have a wonderful atmosphere, are great for photographs and provide a fascinating insight into the Tunisian way of life.

Market Days

Monday: El Jem, Kairouan, Matmata, Houmt Souk
Tuesday: Kebili
Wednesday: Menzel Bourguiba, Gafsa
Thursday: Douz, Le Kef, Nefta, Hammamet
Friday: Nabeul, Tabarka, El Haouaria, Mahdia, Sfax, Midoun
Saturday: Monastir
Sunday: Sousse, Tozeur

Carpets

Carpet-making is one of Tunisia's most traditional crafts dating from as early as the 14th century. While not cheap, they make a handsome and long-lasting souvenir and are readily available all over Tunisia particularly in Tunis, El Jem, Sfax and, of course, Kairouan – the King of the Carpet Centres. Make sure any carpet you purchase has a label of authenticity attached.

The most expensive carpets are knotted, and are priced according to the number of knots per square metre. As a general rule, the firmer the pile and the sharper the definition of the pattern, the greater the value of the carpet and the longer it will last. You can also purchase the woven carpets known as kilims, which usually feature traditional Berber motifs – these are reasonably cheap to buy.

Pottery

Cheap, colourful and very collectible, Tunisian pottery makes the ideal souvenir. Nabeul and Guellala on the island of Jerba are the two big production centres although pottery is sold all over the country. Nabeul's industry dates back to Roman times with many of today's most popular designs and colours (blue and white, and yellow and green) the same as those used 2,000 years ago. Best buys include plates, bowls, vases and tiles which – if you buy several – can make a very attractive wall panel.

Jewellery

Almost every *souq* in the country has its jewellery section. Most Tunisian gold is only 12 or 14 carat while silverwork is often *metal argente* (silver plating). Houmt Souq in Jerba is one of the best places for silver and gold pieces. Common motifs include fishes and the Hand of Fatima, Islam's principal female cult figure who was the daughter of the Prophet Mohammed. The Berber regions of the south specialise in chunky

silver jewellery often set with semi-precious stones. In Tabarka you will find a lot of coral jewellery – but since coral is endangered and protected, it has probably been gathered illegally.

Woodwork and Metalwork

The best wood carving is to be found in Sfax where olive wood is turned into bowls, spoons and chess boards. The tapping of hammers and chisels on brass is a familiar sound in any of the *souqs* where ashtrays, plates and trays are among the most popular items. Craftsman will often offer to engrave a name on pieces bought.

Clothes

Traditional clothes like the *burnous* (a heavy woollen coat) and *chechias* (the traditional red felt hat still worn by many men) can be tempting, but it is as well to question whether it will ever be worn back at home! All the *souqs* sell this kind of souvenir.

Leatherware

Pouffes and *babouche* slippers are good value but be wary of jackets, handbags and belts which can appear to be bargains but need checking carefully for the quality of stitching and overall workmanship. All the *souqs* sell leatherware.

Stuffed camels and bird cages

Lined up in rows outside dozens of souvenir shops – particularly in Port El Kantaoui and Hammamet – few holidaymakers can resist buying a stuffed camel which range from the pocket-sized to those scarily close to the size of the real thing. Equally cumbersome to carry on homeward-bound flights are decorative blue and white bird cages often seen in tourist hotel reception areas where they are used to collect letters and postcards.

Official Shops

ONAT/SOCOPA Shops

In the major tourist centres there is a chain of craft workshops and outlets run by the Organisation National de l'Artisanat Tunisien (ONAT or the National Organisation of Tunisian Craftsmen). The prices are fixed and may be higher than you could pay by haggling, but these shops are less hassle and the goods are generally fairly high quality. The stock tends to be very similar throughout the country, but local produce is always promoted. Opening hours are about 8:30–noon and 4–7PM, but may be shorter in smaller towns.

Bizerte
Quai Khémais Ternane, Old Port
Gabès
Avenue Farhat Hached
Houmt Souq
Avenue Bouguiba
El Jem
Avenue Farhat Hached
Monastir
Rue Abdessalem Trimeche
Nabeul
144 avenue Farhat Hached and 93 Habib Thameur
Sfax
10 rue Lt Hamadi Taj
Tunis
Le Palmarium, avenue Bourguiba

...and Haggle

Bargaining is a way of life throughout the Arab world and, with the notable exception of food and medicines, applies to most commercial transactions. As a general rule, do not express any interest in anything you do not really intend to buy, and always start at a figure that is roughly half of what you would actually be prepared to pay.

Most tourist towns have at least one official shop where prices are fixed (➤ left).

Children's Attractions

Children's Car Seats
Tunisia has no laws concerning the safety of children in cars which means that most rented vehicles and taxis will not have rear seatbelts. If you are concerned about this and planning to rent a car, you will need to inquire in advance. However the reality is that international firms are no more likely than local ones to be able to provide them and it is recommended that visitors take their own strap-in child seats.

Children in Tunisia

Children can be assured of a warm welcome in Tunisia. As with many Mediterranean countries children are treated with great affection – and in Tunisia they represent a sizeable proportion of the population. Latest figures show that more than 50 per cent of the people are under 18 while around one-third are under 14.

But visitors should be aware of the cultural differences which exist in attitudes towards young people. In Tunisia it is not unusual for children to work in shops and markets, to play unsupervised, ride on the back of motorbikes without any sort of protective headgear, and to hitch lifts from complete strangers. This can cause astonishment and concern to first-time European visitors.
They, in turn, can take offence when Tunisians begin fussing over their children, admiring them, occasionally touching them, complimenting the parents and asking what may seem like nosy questions. As always, the best advice is to be relaxed and diplomatic and to remember that half the reason for travelling is for it not to be like home.

Activities for children

Since Tunisia is still developing its package tourism industry there are very few attractions aimed specifically at children such as theme parks and adventure playgrounds. Most museums are not even adult-friendly let alone geared to the minds of children. So most families tend to stick to the beach resorts as children will prefer playing in the sand and sea than touring Roman ruins or walking round *souqs* and markets.
However, the list below gives information on some places designed specifically for children.

Hammamet
Fabiland
This small funfair with rides and slot machines is primarily aimed at the eight to 15 age group.
6km south of Hammamet (close to Hotel Safir) 02 226868 9:30–6:30, summer only

Hergla
Hergla Park
A new go-kart park, featuring a separate track specially for children.
30km north of Sousse
03 251485 Daily 9–7
On-site pizzeria and café

Port El Kantaoui
Acqua Palace
This new waterpark is fairly modest in scale, but it offers a large swimming pool, wave machine, various waterslides and a paddling pool.
9km north of Sousse 03 246728 Daily 9:30–6
On-site pizzeria, self-service restaurant and bar

Tunis
Zoo du Belvédère
This zoo houses a selection of wild cats, birds, snakes and camels.
Park Belvédère 01 281846 9–7 (9–4 in winter)

Buses, camel rides and water taxis
In Hammamet, Sousse, Port

El Kantaoui and Monastir, so-called 'Noddy Trains' – open-sided tourist shuttle buses – are always popular with small children as are short camel rides which are available on many beaches. Watersports are always popular with children and many resort hotels offer tuition for pursuits such as windsurfing. Taking a picnic to another beach by water taxi or making an excursion in a glass-bottomed boat to look at the underwater life is always a popular option.

Pools and playgrounds

One of the reasons why Tunisia has become so popular as a beach destination is that it offers long, warm, sunny days, safe seas and clean beaches which makes it particularly well suited to families. Many of the bigger hotels have separate children's pools and playgrounds. Some also provide children's clubs with qualified helpers arranging day-long programmes of organised activities. In addition, some hotels offer child discounts or will put a child's bed in an adult's room free of charge.

Food and drink

Do not expect to find children's menus except in tourist hotels; normally they will be expected to eat a smaller portion of the adult meal. In resorts, there should be no problems finding hamburgers, hot dogs or pizzas. Pasta dishes also feature prominently on many menus, and the usual fizzy drinks, such as cola and lemonade, are widely available. Some children may find Tunisian dishes too spicy, particularly those containing the fiery *harissa* sauce made from chillies. You can always ask for dishes to be 'sans piquant', but this is not always possible. Salads are often a safe choice as they are invariably based around tuna or eggs. Most children will also enjoy the sticks of crispy white bread which accompany any meal or save up their appetite for a honey-soaked pastry like *baklava* or *makroud.* Finding provisions for a picnic can be a challenge with most supermarkets stocking a very limited range, but markets are where most Tunisians shop and there is always a vast choice of food.

Necessities for babies

Small-size disposable nappies are available at all chemists, although the larger sizes (over 15kg) can be difficult to find. You are not likely to experience problems in finding dried baby milk or bottled and tinned baby food.

Sun precautions

Always remember that the sun is extremely strong in Tunisia, particularly in the summer months. Apply plenty of sunblock and insist they wear wide-brimmed hats, particularly if going on a boat trip: the cooling influence of the wind can be misleading, and the reflective effect of the water makes the rays even more powerful. Make sure you have a dense parasol for the pram if you are taking a baby along.

Public Toilets

There are very few public toilets in Tunisia except at railway stations and airports and these may not be up to the standard usually found in Europe and North America. The best bet is to head to the nearest café or restaurant. Always carry toilet paper as it is rarely supplied. Hand-cleaning wipes can also come in useful.

Sport

Flying Falcons
El Haouaria in the Cap Bon region is Tunisia's main falconry centre. Local enthusiasts catch young peregrine falcons and sparrowhawks in March and April and train them up for an annual Falconry Festival in mid-June. The Club des Fauconniers provides very helpful information for those interested in falconry. Located just outside El Haouaria, it is open from 10-4 daily.

Diving

Tunisia is steadily gaining recognition as a leading scuba-diving destination. The strongest interest is centred on Tabarka which has three major diving sites: Cap Tabarka, Grouper Rock and Tunnels Reef, which is an extraordinary complex of tunnels, caverns, caves and gullies.

Tabarka

Aquamarin
☎ **02 286908**

École de Plongée
☎ **08 644344**

Mehari Diving Centre
☎ **01 79999**

Yachting Club de Tabarka
☎ **08 644478**

Diving is also available at the Port el Kantouai resort, accessible by bus from Sousse (► 70).

Fishing

There is no river fishing in Tunisia but plenty of sea fishing is available. No permit is required and most harbours have boats for hire with or without crew.

Football

Football is the country's national sport and obsession, and is a useful opening conversational gambit with any Tunisian male. All over the country there are organised matches on Sunday afternoons. Tunisia also has its own football league. In Tunis, two local teams – Espérance Sportif and Club Africain – share the El Menzah ground at Cité Olympique.

Golf

Tunisia's temperate year-round climate provides ideal golfing conditions. Many first-time visitors are often surprised by the golf courses in Tunisia which are generally lush and well maintained. A former golf-loving minister of tourism was partly responsible for persuading the government to invest heavily in the sport to provide an added attraction for holidaymakers. Most of the big resorts now have international standard courses. There are no membership requirements and while golfers with their own kit are welcome, those who prefer to travel light will find that everything from clubs to caddies are available for hire – all at very reasonable rates. Many hotels will organise pre-set tee-times and provide complimentary transport to and from courses.

Hammamet

Golf Citrus
Designed and landscaped with six lakes, olive trees and forest, Golf Citrus comprises two 18-hole 72-par championship courses. There is also a schooling course, driving range and putting greens.
✉ **Bir Bou Rebka, 13km west of Hammamet** ☎ **02 226500 Fax 02 226400**

Golf Yasmine
Glof Yasmine is a more intimate course adjacent to Golf Citrus. It offers a single 18-hole course, constructed around twin lakes.
✉ **Bir Bou Rebka, 13km west of Hammamet** ☎ **02 227001 Fax 02 226722**

Port El Kantaoui
El Kantaoui Golf Course
A 36-hole course particularly popular in November, February and March.
✉ Opposite the Hotel Green Park ☎ 03 348756 Fax 03 348755

Skanes
Palm Links Golf Course
Ideally suited to beginners, an 18-hole, 72-par course with a nine-hole schooling course and driving range.
✉ Dkhila ☎ 03 466910 Fax 03 466913

Tunis
Carthage Golf Course
Tunisia's oldest golf club, established in 1927, provides an 18-hole, 66-par course.
✉ Choutrana 2, La Soukra
☎ 01 765 919 Fax 01 765915

Horse riding
There are horses for hire on most tourist beaches and a few coastal hotels even have their own stables. Jerba is particularly well supplied with horses and ponies, and prices are very reasonable. In the Tunis area lessons and escorted rides are available.

Tunis
Club Hippique de la Soukra
✉ La Soukra, 15km north of Tunis ☎ 01 203054

Hunting
The shooting season (Dec–Feb) is centred on the Khroumir Mountains around Ain Draham and Tabarka. The main prey are jackals, foxes, mongooses and wild boar. Permits are necessary and can be arranged by hotels, but it's best to organise these through a tour operator before arrival.

Sailing
Tunisia has some of the best marinas in North Africa which attract wealthy Europeans in the summer and 'yachties' from all over the world in the winter. Facilities are generally high quality and security good. Marinas can be found at:

Bizerte
El Kantaoui
Monastir
Sidi Bou Saïd
Tabarka
Tunis (La Goulette)

Swimming
All major beach hotels have at least one swimming pool, and many now offer indoor pools to attract winter guests. Even if you are not staying in a hotel it is usually possible to use the pool for a small charge. Sea swimming is usually safe and pleasant but jellyfish can be a problem in some areas.

Tennis
Most tennis courts in Tunisia are attached to beach hotels and can usually be used by outside guests as well as residents. Some of the most extensive facilities are at the Club Mediterranée resorts in Jerba and Monastir – but these are closed to non-residents.

Tunis
Cap Carthage
A 30-court complex.
✉ 15km northeast of Tunis
☎ 01 740064

Walking
Ain Draham, Le Kef, Tamerza and Zaghouan are among the main hill-walking centres in Tunisia.

Watersports
One of Tunisia's biggest attractions as a beach destination is that all its major beach resorts are well-equipped with a wide variety of watersports facilities. From hiring a pedalo to more energetic pursuits such as windsurfing, waterskiing, sailing and paragliding, facilities and equipment are available at very reasonable rates. Hammamet alone has more than more than a dozen watersports centres.

Nightlife

Bars

Outside of the main tourist hotels, drinking in most Tunisian bars is confined to early evenings, from around 6 to 9PM. Grimy and smoky, the bars are a meeting place as much as anything else; men of all ages sit together playing cards, smoking *chichas* (through a water pipe) and drinking beer.

The range of night-time entertainment on offer in Tunisia is quite limited. Outside the capital, most evening activities are centred around the tourist hotels, many of which provide free entertainment several times a week. This generally involves local musicians playing easy-listening, internationally known songs – which, after all. is probably what most tourists want after a long day spent in the sun.

Most tour operators will also offer holidaymakers the opportunity to book an evening excursion to a local nightspot for a 'Tunisian Evening' where a specially-tailored version of a traditional Tunisian meal is provided – served with generous amounts of wine and beer. The entertainment on offer normally comprises young women in silk robes and head-dresses performing traditional dances to the accompaniment of folk music. Sometimes there will also be a juggler, snake charmer or belly-dancer – although it is rare to see a performance by a genuine belly-dancer.

Cabaret Dinners

Tunis

Gaston's

Traditional music is played to accompany pleasant food served in a convivial atmosphere.

73 rue de Yougoslavie
01 340417 Fri, Sat evenings

El Mawel

rue Amine Abbassi
01 790321

El Mazar

Live music in a cosy atmosphere with a mix of local people and tourists.

rue de Marseille (above La Mamma restaurant) 01 340423 Nightly from 6–8.30

Mbrabet

Dinner, Berber dancing, traditional folk music and a glimpse of a belly-dancer.

Souk et Trouk
01 261729 Nightly

La Privé

rue de l'Abrabic Saoudite
01 891633

Nightclubs

Bizerte

Hôtel Corniche Palace

route de la Corniche
02 431844

Hôtel Jalta

route de la Corniche
02 420350

Hammamet

Ben's

avenue Moncef Bey
02 227053

Calypso

avenue Moncef Bey
02 226803

Manhattan

Hammamet Sud
02 226226

Nirvana

route Touristique, Hammamet Sud 02 278408

Ranch Club

avenue Moncef Bey
02 226462

Tropicana

route Touristique
02 227200

Mahdia

Club Cesar
✉ Hôtel Thapsus, Zone Touristique ☎ 03 694495

Samba
✉ Hôtel Mehdi, Zone Touristique ☎ 03 681450

Skanès

Hôtel Kuriat Palace
✉ Zone touristique
☎ 03 462200

Hôtel Sahara Beach
✉ Zone Touristique
☎ 03 461088

Sousse

King Nightclub
✉ Hôtel Samara, boulevard 7 Novembre ☎ 02 226699

Marcana
✉ Hôtel Tej Marhaba
☎ 03 229800

Tabarka

Hôtel Abou Nawas Montazah
✉ route Touristique
☎ 08 643532

Tunis

Club 2001
✉ Hôtel El Mechtel, avenue Ouled Haffouz ☎ 01 783200

Le Jocker Club
✉ Hôtel El Hana, 49 avenue Habib Bourguiba ☎ 01 331144

Club Sheherazade
✉ Hôtel Abou Nawas, avenue Mohammed V ☎ 01 350355

Casinos

Casinos have only recently been recognised as another way of attracting tourists and are at present few and far between, but new ones are being built all the time. To gain entry you will need to be over 21 and non-Muslim, so take your passport. Since it is forbidden to gamble with Tunisian dinars, you will need US dollars or some other form of hard currency. Travellers' cheques, Eurocheques and credit cards are also accepted. Opening hours are usually noon–4AM, and the dress code is smart casual.

Hammamet

Casino Emeraude
✉ boulevard Assad ibn el Fourat ☎ 02 278655

Grand Casino
✉ Hôtel Sol Azur, boulevard Assad ibn el Fourat
☎ 02 261777

Jerba

Grand Casino
✉ Sidi Mehrez ☎ 05 757537

Sousse

Casino Club Caraïbe
✉ boulevard 7 Novembre
☎ 03 211777

Cinemas

Cinemas are found all over the country and are one of the most popular forms of entertainment in Tunisia. With only a tiny film-making industry of its own, the cinemas rely largely on a programme of violent American films, kung fu movies and Arabic films, mainly from Egypt.
In Tunis there are more than 20 cinemas, including one at the Hôtel l'Africa Méridien (► 101) which sometimes shows more highbrow French language films. Matinées usually start at 3PM with evening performances at 6PM and 9PM.

Hammams

One of the most leisurely ways of spending an evening or afternoon is by visiting a *hammam* – a traditional steam bath. Found all over Tunisia and popular since Roman times, most Tunisians will visit a *hammam* at least once a week, not only for relaxation and cleanliness but as a place to meet and chat. Visitors keen to learn more about the Tunisians will find a visit to a *hammam* very rewarding. Avoid hotel *hammams* which are a travesty of the real thing.

What's On When

Ramadan
Ramadan is by far the most important festival in any Muslim country and is adhered to by the vast majority of Tunisians. The Koran demands that during the month-long festival (the date of which varies from year to year) no water and no food must pass a Muslim's lips during daylight hours. Some tourists avoid travelling to Muslim countries during Ramadan but it can be quite an exciting time as each evening eating and drinking continue into the early hours. The end of Ramadan is marked with a massive celebration – the Aid es Seghir.

As a Muslim country, Tunisia celebrates a number of national festivals and feast days related to Islam, including the month-long fast of Ramadan (► panel). The dates of these religious events are calculated according to the Muslim calendar which is lunar. Dates are thus eleven days earlier each year. Aid el Adha is a celebration of Abraham's devotion to God who told him to sacrifice his son, but 'stayed his hand' when He saw that Abraham was prepared to follow out the order. A sheep is killed and all the family feast. *Mouled* is a celebration of the Prophet Muhammad's birthday, and Al-Hijra is the Muslim New Year.
The following are among the most popular local festivals:

March–April

Ksars Festival: Berber traditions and folklore,Tataouine.
Festival of Oranges: timed to coincide with the start of the orange-picking season and supported by a programme of cultural events, Nabeul and Menzel Bouzelta.

June

Falconry Festival: falcons trained by villagers take part in a series of competitions to catch partridge and quail before being released into the wild. El Haouaria.
Classical Music Festival: El Jem.
Music Festival: week-long festival of *maalouf* music which was exported to North Africa by Andalusian refugees between the 12th and the 15th centuries. Testour (75km southwest of Tunis).
Ulysses Festival: folklore festival including a re-enactment of the arrival in Jerba of Ulysses, Jerba.

July–August

Festival of Carthage: the biggest cultural festival in Tunisia. Staged within the restored Roman theatre at Carthage and including dance, film, theatre and musical events, Carthage.
Dougga Festival: theatrical performances in the spectacular setting of the Roman theatre within the archaeological site, Dougga.
Festival of Theatre: folk music, dancing and plays, Sousse.
Coral Festival: aimed purely at tourists and at promoting the town's coral shops, Tabarka.
Jerba Folklore Festival: held every other year (even years), Jerba.
International Festival: music, dance and theatre, Monastir.

September

Cavalry Festival: displays of horsemanship, Kairouan.

November

Date Harvest Festival: Kebili.
Festival of Tozeur: oasis folklore and traditions, Tozeur.
International Film Festival: held bi-annually (even years), Carthage.

December

International Festival of the Sahara: attracts up to 50,000 Bedouin, nomads and tourists for camel races and folklore displays. Held in the desert on the edge of town, Douz.

Practical Matters

Before You Go 118
When You Are There 119–23
Language 124

Above: *Tunis has an efficient metro system*
Right: *a decorative postbox in Hammamet*

TIME DIFFERENCES

GMT	Tunisia	Germany	USA (NY)	Netherlands	Spain
→	→	→	←	→	→
12 noon	1PM	1 PM	7AM	1PM	1PM

BEFORE YOU GO

WHAT YOU NEED

● Required
○ Suggested
▲ Not required

	UK	GERMANY	USA	Netherlands	Spain
Passport	●	●	●	●	●
Visa	▲	▲	▲	▲	▲
Onward or Return Ticket	▲	▲	▲	▲	▲
Health Inoculations	○	○	○	○	○
Health Documentation (➤ 123, Health)	▲	▲	▲	▲	▲
Travel Insurance	●	●	●	●	●
Driving Licence (national or international)	●	●	●	●	●
Car Insurance Certificate (if own car)	●	●	●	●	●
Car Registration Document (if own car)	●	●	●	●	●

WHEN TO GO

Tunis

High season

Low season

	JAN	FEB	MAR	APR	MAY	JUN	JUL	AUG	SEP	OCT	NOV	DEC
Season	Low	Low	Low	Low	High	High	High	High	High	High	High	Low
Temperature	6°C	7°C	8°C	11°C	13°C	17°C	20°C	21°C	19°C	15°C	11°C	7°C
Weather	Very wet	Wet	Wet	Sunshine/Showers	Sun	Sun	Sun	Sun	Sun	Sunshine/Showers	Sunshine/Showers	Sunshine/Showers

Very wet · Wet · Sun · Sunshine/Showers

TOURIST OFFICES

In the UK
Tunisian National Tourist Office
77A Wigmore Street
London W1H 9LJ
☎ (0171) 224 5561
Fax: (0171) 224 4053

In the USA
C/o Ambassade de Tunisie
1515 Massachusetts Ave NW
Washington DC 20005
☎ (202) 862 1850
Fax: (202) 862 1858

In Germany
Fremdenverkehrsamt Tunesien
Goethe Platz 5, 60313 Frankfurt
☎ (49) 69 2970640
Fax: (49) 69 2970625

POLICE 197 (National emergency telephone number 197)

FIRE 198

AMBULANCE 481 313/284 808

WHEN YOU ARE THERE

ARRIVING

There are two major gateways. Tunis-Carthage International Airport handles scheduled flights from all over Europe. (There are no direct services from the US). Tunisia's domestic airline TunInter operates flights to Jerba, Tozeur and Sfax. Monastir-Skanès International Airport is used by charter flights.

Tunis-Carthage International Airport

9 kilometres

Journey times

- 20–25 minutes
- 12 minutes

Monastir-Skanès International Airport

5 kilometres

Journey times

- 20 minutes
- 10 minutes
- 15 minutes

MONEY

The monetary unit of Tunisia is the dinar which is divided into 1,000 millimes.There is a one dinar coin and coins for 5, 10, 20, 50, 100 and 500 mills. Banknotes come in 5D, 10D and 20D denominations. The dinar is a 'soft' currency which means that exchange rates are fixed artificially by the govern ment and cannot be traded on world currency markets. It is illegal to import or export dinars so you will be unable to obtain local currency in advance.

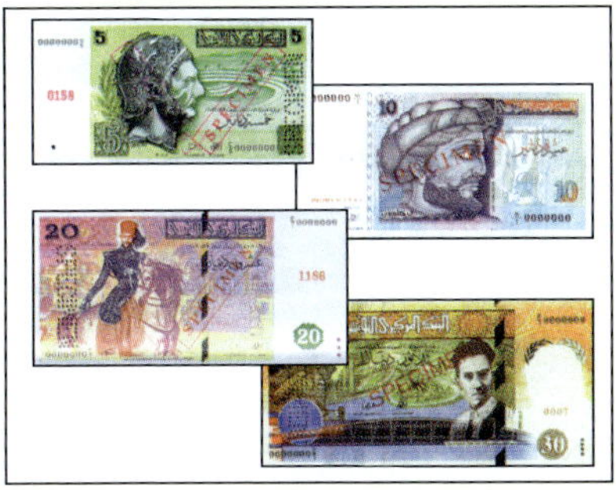

TIME

Tunisia is one hour ahead of GMT all year round which means that flying from Britain in summer there is no time difference while in winter watches have to be put forward one hour.

CUSTOMS

YES

Alcohol:	spirits 1L
Still table wine:	2L
Cigarettes:	200 or
Cigars:	40 or
Tobacco:	400gms
Perfume:	50ml
Toilet water:	1L
Cameras:	2
Video camera:	1
10 rolls of black & white film and 20 rolls of colour	
Jewellery with a precious content:	up to 500 grms.
Musical instrument:	1
A car, motorcycle, caravan or boat.	

NO

Drugs, firearms, ammunition, offensive weapons, obscene material, unlicensed animals.

EMBASSIES AND CONSULATES

UK	USA	Germany	Netherlands	Spain
☎ 01 793322	☎ 01 782566	☎ 01 786455	☎ 01 799442	☎ 01 782217
Fax: 01 792644	Fax: 01 789719	Fax: 01 788242	Fax: 01 785557	Fax: 01 786267

WHEN YOU ARE THERE

TOURIST OFFICES

Bizerte
✉ 1 rue de Constantinople
☎ 02 432897
Fax: 02 438600

Jerba
✉ route de Sidi Mahrez, Houmt Souk
☎ 05 650016
Fax: 05 650581

Monastir
✉ Zone Touristique de Skanès
☎ 03 461205
Fax: 03 463219

Nabeul
✉ avenue Taieb Mehri
☎ 02 286737
Fax: 02 223358

Sousse
✉ 1 avenue Habib Bourguiba
☎ 03 225157
Fax: 03 224262

Tabarka
✉ boulevard 7 Novembre
☎ 08 671491
Fax: 08 673428

Tozeur
✉ avenue Abdul Kacem Chabbi
☎ 06 454503
Fax: 06 452051

Tunis
✉ 31 rue Hasdrubal
☎ 01 845618
Fax: 01 842942

NATIONAL HOLIDAYS

J	F	M	A	M	J	J	A	S	O	N	D
2	1	2	1	2	1	1	1	2	1	1	3

1 January	New Year's Day
18 January	Anniversary of the Revolution
2 February	La Candelaria (Candlemas)
20 March	Independence Day
21 March	Youth Day
9 April	Martyrs' Day
1 May	International Labour Day
1 June	National Day
25 July	Republic Day
13 August	Women's Day
7 November	Anniversary of the Events of 1987

In addition to these secular holidays there are also various Muslim feast days which follow the Gregorian calendar and move backwards by roughly 11 days a year. The biggest holiday is the three-day feast called Aid es-Seghir, marking the end of Ramadan.

OPENING HOURS

○ Shops	● Museums
● Restaurants (lunch)	● Post offices
● Banks	● Pharmacies

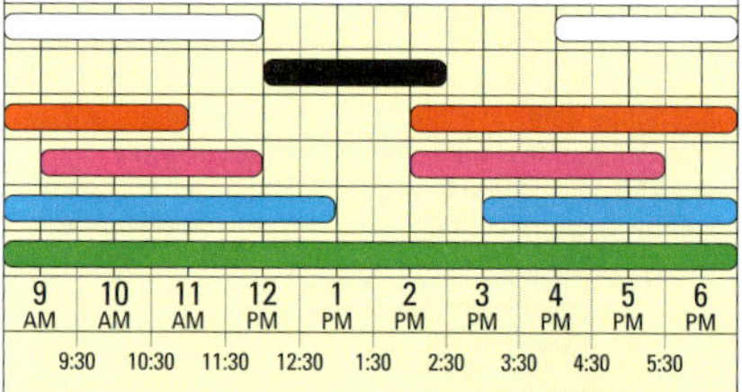

Opening hours can be very flexible according to region, time of year – and even individual whims. In the peak summer months it is not unusual for shops to stay closed for much of the afternoon and then re-open again in the evening when it is cooler. During Ramadan working hours are also generally shortened all round. Many museums and archaeological sites are closed on Mondays. Pharmacies are found in every village and are generally clean and well-stocked with staff speaking fluent French. In large towns, there will be a pharmacy open 24 hours a day.

DRIVE ON THE
RIGHT

TOILETS
BASIC

PUBLIC TRANSPORT

Internal Flights Tunisia's relatively small size means there is not much demand for domestic air travel. The two busiest routes are between Tunis and Tozeur and Tunis and Jerba which is used as a major gateway into Libya. All internal flights are operated by TunInter.

Trains Tunisia's small but efficient rail network is operated by the Societé Nationale des Chemins de Fer Tunisiens (SNCFT). The main line runs north to south from Tunis to Gabes. Three trains daily, whole route; eight services from Tunis to Sousse, six from Tunis to Sfax. Trains offer three classes – second, first and *confort*. Some have air-conditioned carriages.

Buses There is a wide network of bus routes operated by a variety of companies – some of which refuse to recognise each other's existence. Bigger towns usually have a central bus station. Local buses are usually filled to the brim, especially on market days when you may find yourself sharing the journey with chickens or sheep.

Ferries The busiest ferries in Tunisia are those operating between Jorf and Ajim on the island of Jerba. There are year-round services between Tunis and the Italian ports of Genoa and Trapani, with summer connections between Tunis and Naples. Compagnie Tunisienne de Navigation (01 346572) operates between Tunis and Marseille.

Urban Transport Tunis has a *metro leger* (tram) network and a very limited suburban rail service connecting the capital with Carthage and La Marsa. Services are punctual if not exactly frequent. There is also a metro service between Sousse and Monastir which is particularly useful for holidaymakers staying at hotels in Skanès.

CAR RENTAL

Car rental in Tunisia is expensive. Even vehicles from international rental companies can be poorly-maintained, and there are many potential hazards, from people driving at night without lights to pedestrians walking out into the road without looking.

TAXIS

Official taxis are yellow and equipped with a meter. Some drivers will try not to use it, in which case insist, fix a fare in advance or get out and use another taxi. There is a 50% surcharge between 9pm and 6am. In several resorts you can also hire *calèches*.

DRIVING

Speed limit on motorways:
110kph

Speed limit on main roads:
90kph

Speed limit in built-up areas:
50kph

Seat belts are not compulsory and are absent from all but the most modern vehicles. Even then, hardly anyone uses them.

Random Breath Testing: No breath-testing but there are a lot of traffic police and local people are regularly asked to produce their papers. It is almost unheard of for a tourist to be booked unless they cause an accident.

Petrol: Fuel is cheap by European standards and costs the same everywhere. It is sold as super, regular and *essence sans plomb* (lead-free petrol). Although petrol stations are reasonably plentiful, never make the mistake of running short on fuel especially when driving in more remote areas.

Breakdown: Do not expect to be able to call a motoring assistance organisation – although some of the major international car rental companies will provide replacement vehicles and help. Garage mechanics can normally fix most problems. Punctured tyres are common, so if planning a long journey take food and blankets.

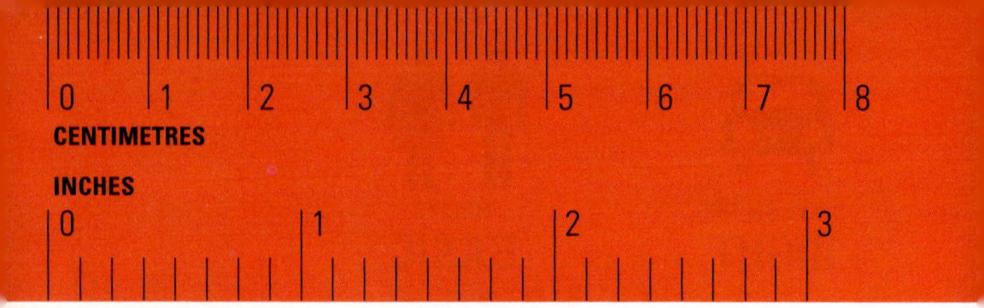

PERSONAL SAFETY

Tunisia is a very safe country with a relatively low crime rate. Sadly, petty thieving is on the increase particularly in busy resorts. Beware of groups of small children distracting you with posies of flowers or cheap souvenirs. To reduce the risk of theft or assault:

- Beware of pickpockets, especially in crowded markets and *souqs*.
- Keep cameras and other valuables in closed bags.
- Do not carry more money and valuables than you need.
- Make use of hotel safes.
- Do not walk alone around *médinas* at night.
- Women should dress modestly, covering themselves when away from the beach or hotel.

Police assistance:
☎ **197** **from any call box**

ELECTRICITY

The voltage is 220/240v.

The power supply in Tunisia is 220 volts although a few more remote areas are still on 110 volts. Sockets accept two-round pin plugs so an international adaptor is needed for most non-continental European appliances. A transformer is needed for appliances operating on 100-120 volts.

TELEPHONES

Tunisia's telephone system is quite efficient. Many households do not have phones, so public facilities are always busy. In major towns and cities look out for Taxiphone offices – easily identified by their bright yellow signs – where there will be several booths under one roof with an attendant to give change. You can make a direct dial international call very easily using one dinar coins. Some shops have public phones, usually indicated by a blue sign.

International Dialling Codes from Tunisia to:

UK:	**00 44**
Germany:	**00 49**
USA and Canada:	**00 1**
Netherlands:	**00 31**

POST

Post offices are known as PTTs (Poste, Telephone, Telegraph) and are well-represented throughout the country. They sell stamps – although these can also be bought from hotels, newsagents and kiosks. Postboxes are generally small and yellow. Postcards and letters to Europe tend to take about a week to arrive.

TIPS/GRATUITIES

Yes ✓ No ✗

Restaurants (if service not included)	✓	10%
Cafes/bars (if service not included)	✓	A few coins
Tour guide	✓	
Hairdressers	✗	
Taxis	✓	Optional
Chambermaids	✗	
Hotel porters	✓	(500mills to TD1)
Theatre/cinema usherettes)	✗	
Cloakroom attendants	✓	(a small coin)
Toilets	✓	Optional

PHOTOGRAPHY

What to photograph: Busy market scenes, the dramatic desert landscape, Sidi Bou Said, camels, mosques, archaeological sites.
What not to photograph: Government buildings, people in uniform, anything military, airports, the Tunisian flag.
When to photograph: Very early morning and early evening.
Where to buy film: It is probably best to bring as much film as you think you will need although most major brands are available from camera shops and souvenir kiosks.

HEALTH

Insurance

Do not try to skimp on travel insurance, which is well worth the investment should problems occur. If you fall ill, all major tourist hotels or a pharmacist should be able to recommend a good doctor – although any treatment would have to be paid for and then reclaimed. If you end up in hospital, immediately contact your insurance company which is there to provide support and advice.

Dental Services

Most tourist hotels should be able to recommend a reputable dentist. Any treatment will need to be paid for and then reclaimed on insurance. It is advised to have a thorough dental check-up before leaving home.

Sun Advice

The sun in Tunisia can be very hot, particularly between June and September in the main beach resorts and in the deep south. Wear a hat, loose cotton clothing and a high factor sunscreen. Drink plenty of bottled water, avoid excess alcohol and caffeine as these aid dehydration – and restrict the amount of time spent in direct sunlight.

Drugs

Pharmacists are knowledgeable and well-respected in Tunisia. Their shops are generally well-supplied although it is always worth checking the date stamp on any medicines which can deteriorate quickly in the heat. Pharmacists can supply drugs for many minor complaints such as sore throat, upset stomach or diarrhoea. Never buy illegal drugs.

CONCESSIONS

Students/Youths: Students with valid identification may get reductions at historical sights and museums. There is a small network of youth hostels in Tunisia, five of them run by the country's Youth Hostel Association. Clean and cheap, there is strict segregation between men and women and a 11PM curfew is imposed. In theory you need to produce a relevant membership card – but it is not always asked for.
Senior Citizens: Tunisia is a very popular destination with older travellers – although they receive no special discounts. Senior citizens tend to be more respected by society than they are in many western countries. It is not unusual for several generations of a family to live together and there is generally much greater interaction between young and old.

CLOTHING SIZES

Tunisia	UK	Rest of Europe	USA	
46	36	46	36	Suits
48	38	48	38	
50	40	50	40	
52	42	52	42	
54	44	54	44	
56	46	56	46	
41	7	41	8	Shoes
42	7.5	42	8.5	
43	8.5	43	9.5	
44	9.5	44	10.5	
45	10.5	45	11.5	
46	11	46	12	
37	14.5	37	14.5	Shirts
38	15	38	15	
39/40	15.5	39/40	15.5	
41	16	41	16	
42	16.5	42	16.5	
43	17	43	17	
34	8	34	6	Dresses
36	10	36	8	
38	12	38	10	
40	14	40	12	
42	16	42	14	
44	18	44	16	
38	4.5	38	6	Shoes
38	5	38	6.5	
39	5.5	39	7	
39	6	39	7.5	
40	6.5	40	8	
41	7	41	8.5	

WHEN DEPARTING

- There are no airport taxes, but you should exchange your spare dinars at the airport as it is illegal to export Tunisian currency. Have your exchange slips with you as you are only allowed to reconvert up to 30 per cent of the total amount of money exchanged in Tunisia.
- Tunisia's airports can be very busy in the summer so allow plenty of time to check-in for your homeward flight.

LANGUAGE

Tunisia is almost bilingual. Although the official language is Arabic, nearly everyone speaks some French and increasingly common among wealthier classes and the business community is for people to speak 'Frarabic'– a rather odd mixture of the two. Not content with two languages under their belt, a lot of young Tunisians are also learning English or German. Tourists can do their bit by learning a few words of Arabic, which is well worth the effort as it usually brings instant friendship.

hotel	*un hôtel*	otel/fondouk
I want a room	*Je voudrais une chambre*	B'gheet beet
Can I look at it?	*Est-ce qu'on peut la voir*	Yoomkin ashoofa?
How much?	*Combien?*	Kaddésh?
too expensive	*c'est trop*	yessir
shower	*la douche*	doosha
open	*ouvert*	mahoul
closed	*ferme*	msaker
bank	*une banque*	bank
post office	*une poste*	bousta/barid
1, 2, 3, 4, 5	*une, deux, trois, quatre, cinq*	wahed, jooj, tlata, arba, khamsa
6, 7, 8, 9, 10	*six, sept, huit, neuf, dix*	setta, seba, tmenia, tse'ud, a'chra
100, 1000	*cent, mille*	mia, alf
the bill	*l'addition*	el-hisaab
fish	*poisson*	samak/huut
meat	*viande*	lahm
vegetables	*légumes*	khodra
fruit	*fruit*	fawakih
water	*de l'eau*	maa
soup	*potage*	shorba
coffee	*café*	kahwa
tea	*thé*	shay
wine	*vin*	sharab
bread	*pain*	khoubz
airport	*l'aéroport*	al-matar
bus	*l'autobus*	autobees
car	*la voiture*	sayara
train station	*gare*	mahata el tran
garage	*le garage*	garage
petrol	*l'essence*	benzeen
puncture	*le crevaison*	tokob
yes	*oui*	naam
no	*non*	la'a
please	*s'il vous plaît*	birabee
thank you	*merci*	shukran
hello	*bonjour*	assalama
good morning	*bonjour*	sabah el khir
good evening	*bon soir*	missa el khir
goodbye	*au revoir*	bislémah
excuse me	*pardon*	samahanee
how are you?	*ça va?*	ashnooa ahwalik?

INDEX

accommodation 100–7
Aghlabid Pools 20
Aïn el Kef 65
air travel 119, 121
Ajim 78
American War Cemetery 36
amusement parks 110
Antonine Baths 26
Archaeological Museum, Nabeul 53
Archaeological Museum, Sfax 72
Association de Sauvegarde de Médina 68
Avenue Habib Bourguiba, Tunis 30

babies' necessities 111
banks 120
bars 114
Bassins des Aglabides 20
Béja 40
Belvédère, Tozeur 87
Berbers 7
Bizerte 29, 40–1
Borj el Kebir, Houmt Souq 80
Borj el Kebir, Mahdia 66
Borj el-Hissar 18
Borg Bourguiba 86
Bourguiba, Habib 11, 14, 68, 86
Bourguiba Mosquée 64, 68
Bulla Regia 42
buses 121
Byrsa Hill 36

cabaret dinners 114
camels 9, 13, 52, 86, 111
Cap Bon 47–55
car rental 121
carpets 108
Carthage 36–8
casinos 115
catacombs 61
Cathédrale de St Louis 36
Cathédrale de St Vincente de Paul 30
Cave of the Bats 50
central Tunisia 59–73
Centre for Arab and Mediterranean Music 25
Centre International Culturel 48
Chebika 82
Chergui 18
children's attractions 110–11
children's car seats 110
Chott el Gharsa 13, 87
Chott el Jerid 13, 82, 90
cinema 75, 115
climate and seasons 7, 118
clothes, traditional 74, 109
coastline 12
concessions 123
Cork Museum 43
customs regulations 119
cycling 75

Dar Cheraït Museum 87
Dar Hammamet 48
Dar Othman 34
dental services 123
departure information 124
desert region 13, 77
diving 12, 75, 112
Dougga 16
Douz 83, 90
Douz Museum 83
drives
  Hammamet to Thuburbo Majus 55
  Sousse to El Jem 64
  Tozeur to Kebili 90
  Tunis to Jebel Ichkeul 45
driving 118, 121

eating out 74–5, 92–9, 111
El Ghriba Synagogue 79
El Haouaria 50, 112
El Jem 17, 64
El Kantara Causeway 78
electricity 122
embassies and consulates 120
emergency telephone numbers 119
entertainment 112–16
Erriadh 79

falconry 112
ferries 121
Ferryville 45
festivals and events 116
fishing 75, 112
fondouks (inexpensive hotels) 107
food and drink 9, 56–7
  see also eating out
football 75, 112
Fort d'Espagne 41

Gabès 83
Gafsa 83
Gammarth 39
geography 7
Gharbi 18
golf 71, 75, 112–13
Gorges de Selja 77, 84
Grande Bain Maure Sidi Bouraoui 61
Grande Mosquée de Sidi Oqba 20
Great Dune 83
Great Mosque, Bizerte 41
Great Mosque, Kairouan 20
Great Mosque, Nabeul 51
Great Mosque, Sfax 73
Great Mosque, Sousse 61
Great Mosque, Tunis 31
Grottes Romaines 50
Guellala 79

Hammamet 47, 48–9, 110
hammams (Turkish baths) 9, 61, 75, 115
Hannibal 14
Hara Seghira 79
harissa (chilli paste) 99
health 118, 123
hill-walking 113
history of Tunisia 10–11
hitch-hiking 74
hookah pipes 74, 97
horse riding 113
Houmt Souq 80–1
hunting 75, 113

Ibn Khaldun 14
Iles Kerkennah 18
insurance 118, 123

Jami'et-Turuk 80
Jebel Ichkeul National Park 19, 45
Jebel Khawi 39
Jemaa ez Zitouna 31
Jerba 78–81
jewellery 108–9

Kairouan 20, 59
kasbah, Hammamet 49
Kasbah Sousse Museum 62
kasbahs, Le Kef 65
Kebili 90
Kélibia 50
Kerkouane 50
Korbous 50
Ksar Haddada 22
Ksar Hallouf 22
Ksar Megabla 86
Ksar Ouled Soltane 22

La Goulette 39
La Grotte des Chauves-Souris 50
La Marsa 39
language 7, 124
Le Kef 65
Le Lézard Rouge 77, 84
leatherware 109
Les Ports Puniques 37
local etiquette 74

Magon Quarter, Carthage 38
Mahdia 66–7
Mansourah 50
maps
  Carthage 37
  Sousse 60
  Tunis 32–3
  Tunisia 28
marhalas (inexpensive hotels) 106
markets 108
Matmata 77, 84
measurements and sizes 122, 123
médina, Hammamet 49
médina, Monastir 68
médina, Sfax 73
médina, Sousse 62
médina, Tunis 34
Metameur 22
Midès 76, 85
Midoun 81

mint tea 95
Monastir 64, 68–9
money 119
Mosquée de Guellala 79
Mosquée de Hammoûda Pacha 34
Mosquée de Sidi Yati 79
Mosquée Sidi Youssef 34
Mosquée des Trois Portes 20
Musée des Arts et Traditions, Monastir 69
Musée des Arts et Traditions Populaires, Jerba 81
Musée des Arts et Traditions Populaires, Tozeur 89
Musée des Arts Populaires et Traditions, Tunis 35
Musée du Bardo 23
Musée de Kalaout el Koubba 62
Musée du Liège 43
Musée National de Carthage 37
Musée Oceanographique, Bizerte 41
Musée Oceanographique, Carthage 37
Musée Regional des Arts et Traditions 73
Musée Regional des Arts et Traditions Populaires 65
Musée Romain et Paléo-Chrétien 38
Museum of Islamic Arts 69

Nabeul 47, 51–3
national holidays 120
Neapolis 52–3
Nefta 24, 85
nightlife 114–15
Noddy Trains 70, 111
northern Tunisia 29–45

Oceanographic Museum, Bizerte 41
Oceanographic Museum, Carthage 37
opening hours 120
Ouled el Hadef 89

Palmery 89
Parc Archéologique des Villas Romaines 38
Parc du Belvédère 35
passports and visas 118
personal safety 122
pharmacies 120, 123
picnic spots 75
police 119, 122
pools and playgrounds 111
population 7
Port El Kantaoui 70–1, 110
postal services 120, 122
pottery 9, 53, 79, 108
public transport 121
Pupput 49

Qasr el-Aïn 24
Quartier Magon, Carthage 38

Raf Raf Plage 12
Ramadan 116
Rass Engelah 12
Regional Museum of Mahdia 66
Remada 86
Remla 18
ribat, Monastir 69
ribat, Sousse 63
Roman aqueduct 55
Roman Caves 50
Roman and Palaeo-Christian Museum 38

Sahara Desert 13
Sahel 59
sailing 113
sales tax 98
salt lakes 13, 82, 90
Sbeïtla 71
Sebastian's Villa 48
self-catering holidays 94
senior citizens 123
Sfax 59, 72–3
shopping 9, 108–9, 120
Sidi Ali el Mekki 12
Sidi Bou Saïd 25
Sidi Bouraoui Baths 61
Sidi Mahrez 81
souqs, Tunis 35
Sousse 59, 60–3
the south 77–90
Spanish Fort, Bizerte 41
sport 112–13
students and young travellers 123
Sufism 85
sun precautions 111, 123

Tabarka 29, 43
Tamerza 86
Tatouine 86
taxis 121
telephones 122
Tell 59
Temple des Eaux 54, 55
tennis 113
Théâtre d'Hadrian 38
Thermes d'Antonin 26
Thuburbo Majus 46, 54, 55
Thuburnica 44
time differences 118, 119
Tinja 45
tipping 98, 122
toilets 111, 121
Tophet 38
Tourbet el Bey 34
tourist offices 118, 120
Tozeur 87–9
trains 121
travel documents 118
troglodyte dwellings 84
Tunis 23, 29, 30–5
Tunnels Reef 43

Utica 44

walks
  Mahdia 67
  Nabeul 51
  Tozeur 88
watersports 75, 113
wildlife 13, 19
women travellers 105
woodwork and metalwork 109

youth hostels 123

Zaghouan 54, 55
Zaouia de Sidi Brahim 80, 85
Zaouia de Sidi Mokhtar 41
Zaouia de Sidi Sahab 20
zoo 110

Acknowledgements
The Automobile Association wishes to thank the following photographers and libraries for their assistance in the preparation of this book.

THE J ALLAN CASH PHOTOLIBRARY 39, 57c; **BRUNO BARBY/MAGNUM PHOTOS** 14b; **MARY EVANS PICTURE LIBRARY** 10b, 14c; **INTERNATIONAL PHOTOBANK** 8c, 91b; **MRI BANKERS' GUIDE TO FOREIGN CURRENCY** 119; **ROBERT HARDING PICTURE LIBRARY** Front Cover (c), 21; **SPECTRUM COLOUR LIBRARY** 51b, 52b, 73b, 79b; **TUNISIA NATIONAL TOURIST OFFICE** 9b, 87a; **WORLD PICTURES LIBRARY LTD** 61.

The remaining photographs are held in the Automobile Assocation's own library (AA PHOTO LIBRARY) and were taken by Steve Day.

Peter Lilley would like to thank Ann Noon of the Tunisian National Tourist Office, London; Jason Nicholls, GB Airways; Panorama Holidays; Abou Nawas Hotels.

Copy editor: Hilary Hughes